AQUARIUS DAWNS:

The Shamanic Artist and the Rise of the Wounded Healer

Also by VerDarLuz

Codex of the Soul: Astrology, Archetypes, and Your Sacred Blueprint

The Art of Partnership: Astrological Essentials for Conscious Relating (online video and audio training)

Praise for Codex of the Soul

"*Codex of the Soul* is a valuable and unique transmission! A clear and poetically expressed explication of evolutionary astrology. VerDarLuz gives the reader numerous tools to take astrology beyond intellectual abstractions and into direct experience. Ideal for students learning the basics, or anyone who wants to understand astrology from a metaphysical perspective. Highly recommended!"

—Benjamin Bernstein, Astrologer/Shaman
Host of This Week in AstrologyPodcast

"I really love how you assembled your book and will recommend it to people who want something with EVERYTHING in it...a wonderful reference book"

—Kristin Fontana, Evolutionary Astrologer,
Host of Guiding Stars astrology podcast

AQUARIUS DAWNS:

The Shamanic Artist
and the Rise of the Wounded Healer

VerDarLuz

Theophany Publishing
Evergreen, CO

Aquarius Dawns:
The Shamanic Artist and the Rise of the Wounded Healer
Copyright©2012, VerDarLuz

Cover Art by VerDarLuz
Design by Clark Kenyon

ISBN: 978-1-62050-174-0

PUBLISHED BY
Theophany Publishing
Evergreen, CO
First Edition, April 2012

Dedication

To all teachers, guides, and mentors who
have lit my path,
and especially to my daimon,
for showing me the way home,
to the center of my soul.

*

The Truth-essence of the master mentor:
I appreciate the opportunity to once again teach
what I have come to learn.

Acknowledgments

I would like to give thanks to the effort of Jenn Jessup and Jesse Chitwood for bringing this book into manifestation with their delicate editor's eye.

I would also like to acknowledge all those shamanic artists who continue to embrace their healing journey and carry the torch across the threshold from one Great World Age to the next.

CONTENTS

And Zarathrustra spoke:
I say unto you, one must still have chaos in oneself to give birth to a dancing star.

—Friedrich Nietzsche

PREFACE

Arise, Wounded Healer

"When I stand before thee at the day's end, thou shalt see my scars and know that I had my wounds and also my healing."
—*Rabindranath Tagore, Indian poet*

I first became aware of my breath when I realized that I may be taking my last.

I was in high school, on my senior retreat, called Kairos, which means "opportunity" in Greek. The most challenging of opportunities was about to transfix my soul. It came shrouded in the cloak of supreme suffering and confusion.

We had come to the towering Redwood forests of the Santa Cruz mountains. It was our first night there and I had just finished my meal, when I began to feel a horrible, stabbing sensation in my chest. Within moments, I found myself gasping for air. Panic began to sink in as I could not catch my breath and underwent the most severe pain in my life. It was as if the wind was being knocked out of me over and over again.

I was taken to lie down in a room. The ambulance was called and a few teachers stood around me, trying to calm me down. Since I went to a Catholic high school, some of those teachers were priests. As I sucked desperately for air, and felt the invisible knife cease-lessly carve open my chest, I began to realize the extreme nature of my predicament. I cannot remember now if I left my body, but I do recall the bewildered shock I felt as I stared into the priest's eyes. I was so confused and so young. What was happening to me? Would I survive? As far as I could tell, I was dying.

Growing up in the Catholic tradition, I was well aware of the "Last

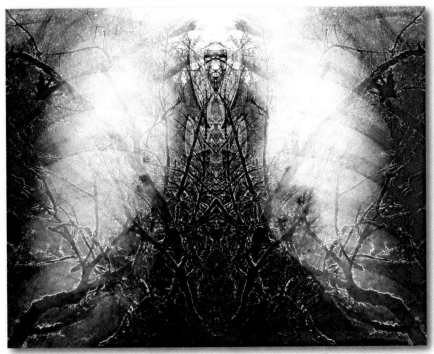

Lungs of Life (2007)

Rites" performed by priests. An ominous feeling came over me as an elder priest held my hand and repeated the Lord's Prayer, the Our Father, over me.

Eternities later, the ambulance at last arrived, and in what I remember as a sort of chaotic frenzy, paramedics attached a device around my thumb to monitor my oxygen levels. When they told me that my oxygen levels were fine, some part of me mustered an internal and ironic laugh from deep within at the fact that I could not catch my breath, and felt that I was quickly departing the earth plane.

They immediately put me in the ambulance, fed me oxygen, and kept close watch of me as we headed away from the mountains into the city and the hospital.

I know now that this incident gave an exorbitant amount of anxiety-soaked gray hairs to both my mother and father, who had to travel over the windy terrain of Highway 17 from San Jose to Santa Cruz to be with me. Shortly after their arrival, we received the x-rays back, to which the doctor commented that I had collapsed my right lung—a spontaneous pneumothorax. I had done nothing to cause this: I never smoked nor had the lung been punctured—it simply just happened.

In the hospital, we waited for my lung to repair itself, which sometimes occurs with a spontaneous pneumothorax. But after ten days of waiting, surgery became required to repair the lung. I was fortunate to have a local doctor who had studied a relatively new surgical operation at the time, involving cameras and actually stapling my lung back together. Had the doctor been unfamiliar with this new procedure, I would be prohibited from high-pressure activities, such as skydiving or scuba diving.

During those two weeks of waiting, surgery, and recovery, I was visited by every person I knew and loved: teachers and priests from my Catholic high school and the church of my upbringing, all of my cousins, aunts, uncles, grandparents, best friends, girlfriend, ex-girlfriend, sister, mom, dad. I will never forget my father's face of compassion while the agonizing fire of potassium shot thru the veins of my hand. His gaze revealed how intensely he wanted to remove my pain, but could not.

Only years later did I fully begin to understand why this experience had to occur to me at such a young age. With understanding cultivated through the arts of meditation, shamanism, and astrology, I realized that the depth of suffering in those delicate moments of my late youth, were an absolute integral element for Love's wings to wrap their warm embrace around me.

Like so many who suffer, I had no ability to change or control my situation. I wondered if I had been chosen—both to experience pain, confusion, and trauma, and also to surrender into the radiant love of my family and friends, the angels of light who taught me the power of compassion.

I did not know it then, but an archetype had seized me in those delicate moments of my youth. The all-encompassing energy of the Wounded Healer gripped hold of me. Eventually, I learned that in fact, I was not "chosen," but *I had chosen* this experience long before this lifetime to teach me to empathize, to move into the boundless space of the sacred heart which unifies us all. From that time onward, the Shamanic Artist would overwhelm, confound, inspire, and enlighten me in my path as teacher, healer, and eternal student of the soul.

At the age of 26, I performed a mushroom healing ceremony with myself that transformed my life. During the journey, after some drumming, I moved into chi kung energy practices and immediately found myself lifting one arm and one leg gracefully up, with slow breath, into the flowing dance of the Crane. As I lifted each arm and leg in rhythm to my breath, I began to feel myself shake and pulse with the energy of this animal. The movement was delivering a message to me.

I had just begun to study astrology, and had attuned strongly to my Mayan day sign of IK, the wind, the messenger, the spirit. In an ecstatic rush of sudden flashes, a series of epiphanies began to unfold. I realized that my Mayan day sign, representing the primal focus for this incarnation, was exactly the same energetic description as my western astrology rising sign, Gemini. The rising sign, or Ascendant, is the outer mask that we wear, our persona, the ship that we must navigate with during this life. One must at all times be free to express their rising sign and will instinctively, impulsively act out this energy. Gemini is the sign of the messenger, the teacher, the communicator, the shapeshifter. In the realization of the correspondence between my Mayan day sign and my western rising sign, a rush of electric impulses shot through me, as if burning into my consciousness my role on the planet.

In those moments, I became Crane—its sense of graceful power, ancient honor, and sincere wisdom. Sinking into the watery underworld, carried by the wind to the heavenly upperworld, and delicately stepping through the earthly middleworld, the crane is a bird of air, land, and water—a shapeshifter, like Gemini, able to exist in many environments and dimensions of consciousness.

Chi Kung and Tai Chi were originally expressions of a kind of Taoist shamanic alchemy. By observing the movements in nature and then mirroring those movements, one invokes the spirit of an element, of geography, or of an animal. As I moved the crane through chi kung, I began to cry as Crane informed me as to what had truly occurred when I was 17: the purpose of my lung collapse was to initiate me into the path of the messenger.

I had suffered without breath and without voice. This same wound would allow me in the following years to heal and teach others through language and breath—as an author, speaker, counselor, songwriter, and Rebirthing Breathwork facilitator.

The word for breath in virtually all spiritual and religious traditions corresponds to "spirit," or "life-force." Literally, Crane had entered my energy body at that moment, and the force of what I was to communicate, what my soul had for lifetimes been sharing with others, was so strong as to collapse my lung, the mechanism of breath and the vehicle for life.

I could feel there were other bird-energies present in me, yet unrealized, who years later, would continue to inform my role as astral bard and shamanic counselor—Owl, Hawk, Blue Jay—all beings with distinct messages and spirit-reminders for me when they now appear in my life.

Around the time of this transformational medicine ceremony, I was familiarizing myself with the profound work of religious scholar Mircea Eliade on the topic of shamanism. I became aware that my near-death experience at such a young age compared to the illnesses and dismemberments of initiate shamans in indigenous cultures. The "spontaneous aspect" of my lung collapse also suggested forces at play from the spirit world. Like native shamans, I was to bring healing and multidimensional perspectives to others' lives.

In Ted Andrew's *Animal Wise Tarot* deck, he associates Crane with the hierophant, who links us to cosmological and spiritual understanding, and for me, to the lineage of astrologers and shamans.

The sense of being woven into a vast and luminous web of life humbled me to the preciousness of this life. It awakened a commitment to celebrating life with more passion, to serving with more compassion, and to living in abundant radiance with divine purpose.

The astroshamanic lense is both zoom and panoramic: it challenges you to pry open your perception into your multidimensional nature. Each of us has along the way recognized a repeating wound, amidst the magic and mystery of life. Since 2004, I have been consistently blessed to find astrology and shamanism to be mutually supportive languages in navigating the soul's toils, troubles, and triumphs.

My Wound and Healing in the Writing of this Book

Of all the possible books I could read, the first text in Western Astrology that found me was Melanie Reinhart's *Chiron and the Healing Journey*. Reinhart's exploration of the Wounded Healer spoke to every cell of my being. I did not yet understand the true significance of Chiron in my own life. Nor did I grasp at the time the information that I share in this book: the Wounded Healer's importance as the leading archetype bridging the Piscean and Aquarian ages and this shamanic mentor guiding us through the Galactic Center portal of 2012 and the succeeding decades.

Chiron says,

> *I am not only a wound which must be healed. I am a part of your consciousness that uniquely perceives and languages the world. I represent an original lens, an individual filter from a higher source that can be grounded into an important teaching, idea, innovation, or guidance.*

Irony is part of the Wounded Healer's formula. Through means which are *chironic,* we are often blessed with an ability to help others in ways in which we cannot help ourselves. In my own chart, with Chiron conjunct Mercury—planet of thought, communication, and perception—my knowledge and lens on reality, as well as my technologies of communication, could be both enlightening and awakening to others but bring debilitating struggle, suffering, and communication/technology challenges to me.

With both of these planets in the vast archetypal ocean of the twelfth house, I at times felt like the gods and the muses, Urania (astronomy and astrology) in particular, were strangling or drowning me, allowing in more inspiration than could leak out one breath at a time. My mind was not built as a linear machine. Rather, the archetypes swim with each other in those vast mythical seas, they swing between vines, twisted and serpentine. So how could I put my thoughts "in-formation" for others to dance with?

History was bleeding through my pores, but not the stale history of rote memorization, the kind meant to perpetuate the propaganda machine of the USA. No, a new understanding of Time had been erupting in my consciousness since astrology seduced me with her exquisite tango. I began to comprehend that the energetic essences of events would recur every time the same planets aligned in a similar configuration. Thus, the god Chronos repeated himself. Time updated his form.

How could I speak of the emergence of the Wounded Healer as the primary archetype of our age, without unfurling the epic scroll of the doctrine of the Great Aeons, the vast 2,250 year epochs of time? And to fully elucidate the architecture of this peak in transition between the Piscean and Aquarian ages, how could I not describe the apex moment of the 2010s, a decade whose archetypal stew steams over with resonances from the pivotal shifts of the 1960s, 1930s, and the late 1840s and early 50s? And perhaps most importantly, how could I not promote the Wounded Healer at the turning of the ages as the Shamanic Artist, and the wise educator—a revolutionary mystic determined to guide parents and teachers on how to raise individuated beings of light, love, peace, and compassion?

This messenger's mission has been both impossible and absolutely necessary.

It has been bestowed to me as a gift, and noosed around my neck as a curse.

Healing is a messy act—paradoxical, but poetic.

Chiron, the Wounded Healer, reveals the power of the shaman's call, a vocation which you cannot ignore, like the vision which shakes raw the artist's eye, the song that spirals through the heart of the musician, the innovation that bedazzles the future engineer, the light that dances in the hands of the healer.

The technological challenges I faced while writing this book compelled me to ask if I was repeating karma. My own past life wounds and birth trauma scars of failed initiations and incomplete creative acts, forced me into a state of urgency and frustration with the human limits of space and time. Would those wounds manifest again in another project begun but abandoned, in another creative child left orphaned?

Yet I knew I was not alone. I felt all around me this same spirit of Promethean revolutionaries chained to the stones of old wounds, and to the burdens of spacetime boxes, bills to pay, and increasingly inept authoritarian structures.

And I knew that I had to do it differently. My creative *process* is the final product, and this process is perpetual. Thus, poetry, song lyrics, dialogues, and hyperlinks to songs, images, and video are used throughout the text to illustrate certain characteristics of the Wounded Healer and Shamanic Artist

In Part 1, we introduce the concept of the Shamanic Artist through journal and personal storytelling. We then investigate the shift of the Ages from Pisces to Aquarius, the role of the artist and light-worker in this pivotal transition occurring now.

In Part 2, we discuss the relationship between the Mayan prophecies of 2012, the Galactic Alignment window, the Aquarian Age, and the emergence of this new guiding archetype: the Wounded Healer. By exploring Chiron's myth and symbolism, we learn about the important themes which lay the foundation for the transformation of society. These include the motifs of the orphaned and exiled self, ancestral healing, a hybrid, shamanic identity, the artist's struggle with the muse, the connection to a higher self, and an appropriate relationship to our fate.

We also apply a lens from alchemy, Buddhism, and other spiritual lineages to understand the healing invitation upon us now. We then discover how the Wounded Healer is now appearing in popular culture, such as in the world of personal coaching and in the art of film.

In Part 3, we reveal the astrology of Chiron by sign, house, and aspect, and the importance of locating the Wounded Healer in your personal birth chart.

***

At the dawn of the Aquarian Age, you must take your evolution into your own hands. And this evolution requires a self made whole: the one who embarks unconditionally on the healing journey.

In this book I describe the importance of unveiling the hidden crevices of our soul, the labyrinthine passages that lead to the treasure—the alchemical gold of a luminous, blissful life filled with delicious gratitude and humble service.

It is my hope that this will begin a series of books about the quest of the shamanic hero at the emergence of the Aquarian age. And yet, as we observe the pace of the world shifting through us and accelerating around us, we cannot guarantee a tomorrow. Our promise is only this moment's breath.

My naked truth is that I, as the messenger brother of Wind, do not know if or when another book will happen, or if it should, or in what form. A non-fiction work? A fictional memoir? A merger of fiction/non-fiction/poetry/song/dance/video? I am learning to make peace with the knowledge that I am all of these creative voices. And I am so much more. And, on the most primal level, I am none of them.

One of the great challenges for the artist and lover of today involves labels, genres, and definitions. Thus, a major test is to let go of attachments to the form of our creative self-expression. Instead, we are asked to cultivate our intuition—to teach, share, and inspire through whatever tools are most suitable.

Hopefully, as you read, you will feel your own healing and creative journey resonate through the myth and the medicine of Chiron, the Wounded Healer. You are creative beyond comprehension and I hope this information will activate and spark the Divine Creator within.

I invite you to stay open to these didactic confessions, this visionary non-fiction, this journal torn inside out, this shamanic artist dismembered, putting himself and this world back together, one broken shard at a time, brushstroke by brushstroke, painting the zeitgeist with the blood, bone, and song of stars.

We have been suffering in our individual games, boxing with egos against the ropes. But we have been suffering together.

And we have been rising, towards the One Light that electromagnetizes us.

The Wounded Healer has been rising, on the spiral path of ascension.

You are not alone.

Because You are One, remembering.

Re-member. Join me and let's puzzle piece ourselves back together. The stars are singing, their chorus faint for centuries, now echoes arkastral. We can no longer turn away from the opera's open curtain. This alchemical opus is ours to compose.

PART 1

SONG of STRUGGLE:
The Shamanic Artist Awakens

If the soul is to be truly moved, a tortured psychology is necessary. For the soul to be struck to its imaginal depths so that it can gain some intelligence of itself... pathologizing fantasies are required...these patholo-gizing fantasies are precisely the focal point of action and movement in the soul.

—James Hillman

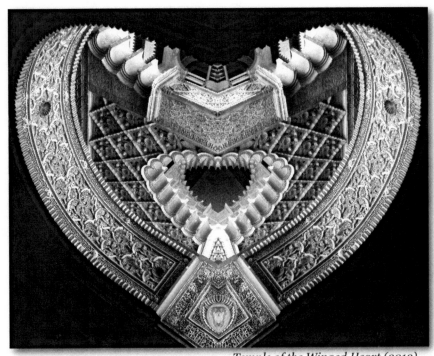

Temple of the Winged Heart (2012)

To teach the archetype of the Wounded Healer,
I offer up my own wounds:
confessions like blown kisses to you
from the heart of my journal.
Two question marks, one reversed,
shape the questing heart.
That interrogation is this book.

3/9/11 - Journal Entry

Today I write about information overload as one of the major shadow components of the emerging Aquarian Age. I smile at this, a melancholy and bitter smile. I laugh at this, but my grin is sour apple candy, sad to admit that this very same information overload is what will prevent people from reading this work to begin with. It's also what makes me write in vast ellipses of repetition.

And because I have been writing this book for so many years, it's scattered, like lost neurons in the mycellial brain of my hard drive. I watch my mind begin to write about a subject. Then I will search it on my Macbook's spotlight. I find what I've just typed, written one or two years ago in a completely different file. So I realize that I've just been rewriting this book over and over again.

So if I continue to amass more information, and begin to initiate more sections of the book, then I will never complete the book. Thus, I am simply repeating the trauma of other lifetimes—the burnt and drowned books, the messenger in me killed, message undelivered. The book represents all these fragmented parts of my soul.

I can't handle this awareness. Distract myself. Check the email.

Oh shit. Pinwheel of doom over Safari. NO! The machine's going to freeze again. Quick, save all the open docs in Word....

....Lost it. I had to "Shut Down" again. Shut Down. This is what happens to my spirit each time my computer dies and enters the domain of the Underworld.

Don't react. Yesterday I wrote, "In the Buddhist practice of Tonglen, we avoid doing the habitual behaviors which always paralyze us: the compulsion to push away that which is painful and cling to that which is pleasurable. Tonglen reverses this pattern. Instead, when it's painful we breathe it in, own it, and allow ourselves to be touched by it without being torn apart by it....."

Don't react. Don't feed it. But it's happening every other day now, sometimes twice a day.

"You have to have a backup strategy," says my friend Prometheus.

Backup. Strategy. Hard drive as the extension of the mind. Hard drive fails = losing one's mind.

This must be a repetition. This must be a repetition and a compulsion. Like Freud said: the wound, costumed in the dense colors of shadow, will repeat ad nauseum, until you choose to heal it.

But what kind of past lives with this repeating pattern (or maybe it's not past, just current in another dimension—the multiverse theory of physics?) as a recorder or transcriber, when at any moment, my entire work could be lost or destroyed?

Were the books burnt during an invasion of some sort? But in a sudden invasion, I would not feel the consistent anxiety. No, it'd have to be some secret writing I was not supposed to be doing, and then was caught. An occult order? A brotherhood of light, forced to hide in the shadows? A path of ascension from the dark heart of the dungeons? Our breath, whispering the message of the Holy Spirit like a serpent wind over candle flame?

Yes, this resonates. Go there. Soar or Swim. But grab the drum and ride the uninterrupted breath. Sound the sky pegasus or Poseidon's ocean chariot and journey through the whirlpool of your karmic vortex....

The Shamanic Artist: A Dialogue

"Success is to be measured not so much by the position one has achieved in life, but by the obstacles he has overcome"
—Booker T. Washington

"That happiness endures which comes from the grinding together of anguish and ecstasy and from the intensity of the grinding. That knowledge is true that comes from the searching into doubts and beliefs, and from the depth of the searching."
—Zicheng Hong (15-16th C), Ming China, from: Discourse on Vegetable Roots

V: You'll never guess what happened to me at the Gathering of the Hearts last Valentine's weekend.

Guiding Friend: Tell me.

V: There were about 40 of us gathered in the yoga studio. Everyone was beautiful, dressed in white. We had just finished our opening circle and the passing of the medicine. Everyone said a special blessing over the medicine and we all took it together, immediately following the teaching from *A Course in Miracles*. I was up next, preparing to perform a shamanic dance invocation. I came out with my Owl mask and barely anything on my body. I stood in mountain pose until my friend hit play on my computer. It was one of my original compositions—really intense orchestral strings, haunting. I slithered through the space, with bone and feather, and at the moment of peak intensity in the piece, the energy of the room froze at the sound of a huge crash. At that moment, I didn't know what was happening, so I improvised and fell to the ground, like I had been slain in some dramatic theatrical death scene. I stayed there for a few minutes, hearing some shuffling in the room. I slowly stood up, grabbed my guitar for the second half and then performed another deep journey as originally planned. I finished my set, out of breath.

A few minutes later, I moved to the back of the room to my computer, still uncertain what had happened. Then Time stopped.

Guiding Friend: What was it?

V: I looked down to see that a huge dent had been carved into the top of my computer, near the mouse.

GF: Shit.

V: I could move the cursor but I couldn't close or open any windows. I shut down the computer. When it tried to restart, only a flashing hard drive appeared.

GF: Oh man.

V: At that moment, something took over and I began to watch myself. I asked a friend to come out in the hall with me to help me survive the shock of what had just happened. I kept feeling another spirit there as I witnessed myself. I kept hearing all these Buddhist lessons about equanimity and impermanence and non-reaction so you don't create new karma. But then, I also was hearing my regression therapy teachers talking about how trauma occurs and we shut down at that moment because we can't handle the energy. And then that energy gets stuck within us and collapses the vitality of our essence. This, in turn, fragments our souls.

So I was watching myself vacillate between doing some huge primal scream cathartic release or very calm non-reactivity. And I never really chose, I just watched. There was a triangulation of energy between the "me" experiencing it, the "witness," and what I felt was another spirit there, almost like it was conducting the whole damn thing.

If we were at a church and that had happened, they would have called it a demonic event. Something else was going on. The synchronicity was too profound. During *my* song that *I* was dancing to, the vibration of the speaker was so intense that it fell onto *my* computer and destroyed the hard drive?! That's fucked up. It's like I did it to myself. Like some kind of technological suicide. I can't really grasp it, it's too much.

GF: Take a deep breath.

V: Huh, yeah. I put in a new hard drive a few days ago, but now every day the computer dies. The pinwheel of doom appears and I know I'm going to have to restart.

GF: I know this all feels crazy, but keep breathing through it. You didn't think you could write about the Wounded Healer without facing and embracing your own wounds, did you?

V: It feels like a sick joke, a poetic paralysis. I've been struggling with what to communicate and getting lost in all my notes, and asking just what can manifest NOW? Yes, I know it's that Saturn square my Sun, demanding some form for my self-expression. And now as Saturn is finishing up my 5th house, demanding creative product.

GF: But all creativity is ultimately about the creator *becoming*, not the product. I want to give you this quote, maybe it will help: "In the process of creation, in the production of the opus, in this path, your purpose should be unassuaged, but your will should be delivered from the lust of result."

V: Yes. Sometimes I feel the intensity of this lust as I project myself out into my death-moments. You know, perceive this moment from the Death Bed Life Review. Like when Nietzsche talked about Eternal Recurrence: that you should live each moment as if you were forced to live it over again and again. And how easily all the stories of incompletion will catapult me into another suffering rebirth. Sometimes I think, "If I have so many possible projects and books now, what will it be like in those final moments, whenever they come?" I will have to make peace and let them go.

GF: You can't own anything when you die. You can't take anything with you. Fall in love with the process, and find your bliss there. This is where the wisdom lives and sprouts.

V: I feel like I've been so damned patient, waiting for so many lifetimes.

GF: Let go of attachment to results, you know, like in the Bhagavad-Gita when it says "Be not attached to the fruits of your actions..."

V: It's so different than songwriting. I can compose a song in one evening, and refine it over a few days. I can sculpt its form, I can carve its body, and then it can be shared with the world. Writing a book is totally different.

GF: Listen. You need to be careful with who you think is doing what. When you are on your death bed, letting *your* projects go, when you think *you* are writing the songs or the books, you must realize that you are only a conduit. And your special creative talent is just that you've finally learned to get out of the way enough for the channel to open.

V: I know. I'm trying to get out of the way. But in this lifetime, and I'm sure in others, it feels like almost but not quite. It feels like I have to prove to myself my experiences are real and didn't just exist inside of me.

GF: What difference does it make if it was just inside of you? It's like mystical experience or epiphany. You can't prove that to anyone. You're not supposed to. Think about all the wise Sufis, the Yogis who dwelled in the forest of India and composed the Upanishads, the Taoist masters, or the anonymous author of the Cloud of Unknowing. They did not need validation from outside themselves to ascend into Truth.

V: But creations, ideas, visions, songs, they're supposed to be experienced by others. It feels like I'm not giving back, not using my talents or being the bodhisattva. The messenger is not the messenger if the message isn't delivered. It's like narcissistic self-absorption to hold on to what you know. Or I feel victimized if my technology prevents me from sharing my story or my art.

GF: No. The greatest thing you can do in walking your path is to not allow the ego to control the process by observing the traps and games of the mind. Your relationship to your sacred work IS the test of your spiritual evolution. Your mind is re-creating your karma. Ultimately you have to realize it doesn't matter if the world sees it or not: it matters if you are transformed through your art. I bet whoever thought the alchemists were actually trying to make gold probably called them all crazy and deficient when no physical gold was produced. But the real alchemists, the pioneers of the spirit, knew that the Opus would evolve their entire vibration, and had nothing to do with anything superficial.

V: But how do we create unconditionally? I keep second guessing myself. Which project now? It's all one to me, hard to separate. And what's the message of the broken machine?

GF: To give birth, you have to become a child. You have to play with it. There's many a game played by kids who just abandon it for something else fun. You should be having fun with whatever is channeling through you. Even if it hurts, remember to play.

HALO

Angel
I'm strangled by my Halo
and I don't know
which way
to Grow

Where's your whisper
to guide me across the Milky Road
a Voice to help me
climb the starry rope?

Planetary puzzle
in the mirror
seduces me
towards the black hole
sacred celestial
ever-spiraling
womb-whole

Theres no hiding
from heaven's holy ghost,
too many paths open, o-pen
for this messenger's throat

To find my way
back Home
Give me a Light to Follow
Some old Star to Fall Low

Holding on
Only grasps at hope
But letting go
Becomes the Unicorn,
The Wing'd Unicorn...

(Follow LINK http://soundcloud.com/verdarluz/halo to song)

Halo (2006)

CHAPTER 1

From Piscean Projection to
Aquarian Shamanifestation

When an experience repeats in our lives, and especially when we suffer due to this experience, we naturally apply the magnifying glass to discover the causes of our painful condition. When plowing the depths for the roots of our suffering, we must gallop, like the centaurs, straight into the heart of the dark forest. We weave through our labyrinth arriving back in the traumas of childhood or other lifetimes, or in unresolved relationships, and notice there a pattern of the sacred wound, etched into our souls.

We can be both intimidated and overwhelmed by forces we discover lurking in the swampland forests of the unconscious. Especially poignant in the closing decades of the Piscean Age are the interrogations of the wounded Piscean and Virgoan aspects of ourselves. These polarity signs both play the role of hopeless victim, and disillusioned martyr.

The Virgo part of us challenges the whole possibility of healing with the question, "Why again? I thought I healed this. Why won't this pattern end? What's the point, because I'm permanently scarred anyway?" On the other hand, our Piscean aspect asks, "Well, if my soul intended this, and it's all supposed to be perfect and divine because it's happening, then why bother do any healing around it?"

During one of my initial rebirthing sessions, I posed this question to my rebirther. Below is a paraphrased summary of the response, which acutely describes the Wounded Healer's ambitious journey.

Although you may have chosen it on the soul-level, there are patterns in your life flowing out from that birth imprint which will cause you pain and suffering. The purpose of doing healing work around this imprint is to become conscious of those patterns, why your soul chose this birth experience for your evolution, and how to move forward without the same level of suffering. It's the same with any wound which you become conscious of. As you integrate the awareness of the wound and its larger purpose to serve you and the planet, then you will not have to experience as much pain on your journey because you offer back your suffering as a healing service. This is how what was formerly pain becomes a sacred wound, and how that wound transforms from a curse to a gift.

The Pisces-Virgo Axis: From Delusion to Union

We are currently in the closing centuries, perhaps even decades of one Great Aeon, the 2,250 year long cycle of the Piscean Age. But it is important to know that as one age closes and another begins, the contrast increases between the shadow and luminous expression of the Piscean energy, as well as Pisces' opposite sign, Virgo. A sign of the zodiac is an archetype—a primal pattern of energy. A sign is always balanced by its polarity energy. Thus, the opposite sign of the Age will also demonstrate both the negative shadow and the healing medicine necessary for wholeness. If those existing in the Piscean age have not integrated both Piscean and Virgoan qualities as well, they will demonstrate the shadows of both; thus, preventing the embrace of the emerging Aquarian-Leo axis of consciousness.

When my computer was crushed, when my hard drives failed repeatedly on me, when multiple recording and composing gear would get lost or broken, I applied a technique from past-life regression therapy. I repeatedly said to myself, "It feels like....It feels like..." until what spontaneously erupted was the statement, "I can't deliver my message, which means I can't live my life's purpose. So it feels like I should not be alive."

Arriving at this sentiment can create a sense of victimhood because I am here, but unable to do or fulfill my purposes here.

The ego always wants to know WHAT TO DO. This is the darker aspect of Virgo, with its pages and pages of impossible to finish "to do lists," or with its overly critical eye attuned to all the wrongs and imperfections which must be fixed.

But our most important task is simply to witness *how we think*, and to observe how what we think affects our spiritual, emotional, and physical health. For, as the Buddha taught, from our thoughts shall arise our actions. And if we perceive ourselves as these separate and limited beings, then we will never be able to do enough, never do it well enough, never heal, and so we will perpetually feel guilt, victimization, or martyrdom.

But if we can recognize the truth of our inseparability and original Wholeness, the luminous Virgo aware of its interconnectedness along the web of life, then we are complete in our Oneness, and therefore we are innocent. In our innocence, we do not have to accomplish anything, we can simply **BE**. The healing that can come from Piscean presence, acceptance, and surrender can lead us to remember the wholeness that never really left. This is the mystical ability of Pisces to receive the divine perfection of all things at each moment.

When the speaker fell and crushed my computer, I entered a dangerous battlefield. Should I stay with the painful energy and drop the storyline, or dive deep into the story and re-interpret its meaning?

Either way, the repeating wound hovers like a shadow around us, whispering into our ear that avoidance is not an option.

The art of the Wounded Healer, and the healer as shamanic artist, as we shall discover, requires both abiding in equanimity with our suffering *and* cathartically embracing the story, in order to re-write it. This is our major test at the end of the Piscean Age. How are we challenged?

Often, instead of truly abiding, and riding with the uncomfortable energy, we try to avoid the repeating wound. We prefer to fall into a kind of intoxicated distraction, in which we don't actually deal with the causes of our suffering. The media, internet, videogames, facebook, bars, clubs, and general busy-ness without self-reflection all give us plenty of opportunity to seemingly "escape" our wound.

But sometimes we do recognize the wound, and fear the healing journey. So then we take one of two paths. First, we may seek out a messiah or redemptive savior in anything in our environment—a guru, a counselor, an alcoholic binge, a move abroad, cosmetic surgery, a sexual partner, the "perfect marriage", a Second Coming, an alien salvation, etc.

Alternatively, instead of owning the wound, we may project that wound onto others around us. These are the dramas that play out daily in the world of politics, news, and mainstream media, and consistently plague our interpersonal relationships, where blame and illusions can dominate.

These Piscean pitfalls increasingly threaten us during the pivotal decades of Neptune's journey through Pisces, between 2011-2024. During this time, the veil will be most thin between this dimension and others. Reality becomes more liquid and surreal. Any sense of ground or anchor is washed away in the undertow impermanence of tidal swells. Thus, projections, fantasies, and distractions may seduce us into avoiding the healing journey.

A Course in Miracles elucidates the real mechanism behind our projections: the ego's desire to remain separate. This is our major obstacle to the goal at the end of the Piscean Age: to awaken to unity and remember our Wholeness.

> *Any split in mind must involve a rejection of part of it, and this is the belief in separation. The Wholeness of God, which is His peace, cannot be appreciated except by a whole mind that recognizes the Wholeness of God's creation. By this recognition it knows its Creator....what you project you disown, and therefore do*

not believe is yours. You are excluding yourself by the very judgment that you are difference from the one on whom you project....Yet projection will always hurt you. It reinforces your belief in your own split mind, and its only purpose is to keep the separation going. It is solely a device of the ego to make you feel different from your brothers and separated from them....Projection and attack are inevitably related, because projection is always a means of justifying attack.

But, if we change our perception, we may stop our vicious attacks and realize the potential at the end of the Piscean age. This is a test to perceive ourselves as the extensions and reflections of divinity, and therefore, perfect, rather than separate and flawed.

Every ability of the ego has a better use, because its abilities are directed by the mind, which has a better Voice...The Holy Spirit begins by perceiving you as perfect. Knowing this perfection is shared He recognizes it in others, thus strengthening it in both. Instead of anger this arouses love for both, because it establishes inclusion.

What opportunities do we have to reflect this perfected perception of the Holy Spirit? Worldwide meditations and synchronized, synesthetic festivals, merging all senses will become more of the dominant paradigm under Neptune in Pisces, (2011-2014) increasing our awareness of the Unified Field. Events which blend the aesthetic wonders of visionary and transpersonal art, global music, and evolutionary, integral education will proliferate, igniting, inspiring, and uniting us.

But the unified celebration of the divine imagination can only become possible if each of us consistently embraces the healer within, refining oneself daily, amidst the ecstatic distractions of Neptune in Pisces.

For those who open to the increasing spiritual light, they will be compelled to discover and heal their multidimensional soul. Because more of us will gather together collectively under this transit, in person and virtually, we will naturally be rediscovering many of our soul mates, who have travelled through space and time to meet us once again. These kindred reconnections will reveal more aspects, some wounded and incomplete, of our soul-stories which must be integrated and made whole.

On the deepest possible levels, there will be a mass remembering like never before. Thus, a return to the primal myths will continue to filter into our media.

We will be invited, as a global culture and as individuals, to discover the true origins of who we really are. The psyche itself—its dreams, its archetypes, its imagination—will become the necessary terrain for exploration. What we discover on this journey will help us all compose a new meta-narrative filled with an Aquarian cast of characters which will include the unleashed creator, the humanitarian visionaries, and the liberated tribes of innovators, adaptable in applying their genius towards the freedom of all.

The Virgo Crisis

If you bring forth what is within you, what you bring forth will save you.
If you do not bring forth what is within you, what you do not bring forth will destroy you.
—Gospel of Thomas, Saying Number 70 - Yeshua, the Christ

If instead of avoiding it, we choose to enter the story of our wounding, we may run into the obstacles of Pisces' opposite sign Virgo: the guilt complex. On a fundamental level, at the end of the Age of Pisces, we are dealing with this pervasive existential guilt forever lurking as background noise. We ask, "What did I do wrong to cause this suffering I feel?" If we don't ask this question, then Virgo wounds manifest as the repressive energy which gets stuck in our physical and energetic bodies, causing us much of the ailments we suffer today. This struggle often compels us to walk the twisted labyrinth of the healing journey.

The Pluto in Virgo generation, born between 1956-1971, are most acutely aware of a kind of nagging, insistent pressure to always work on themselves, to improve, to analyze, to fix it all. This can create lives of enslavement, criticism of self and others, inferiority complexes, and self-denial. But this generation is also seeding the Virgo medicine, which we see sprouting all around us: the path of the sacred servant, the mentor, guide, ecologist, and the disciplined practitioner of the healing arts—Yoga, chi kung, massage, energy work, holistic nutrition, and more.

At the close of the Piscean Age, the Wounded Healer has become attuned to the reality of soul-loss. The Virgo aspect within us recognizes the need to recover one's lost soul fragments.

> *I am not a mechanism, an assembly of various sections.*
> *And it is not because the mechanism is working wrongly,*
> *   that I am ill.*
> *I am ill because of wounds to the soul, to the deep emotional*
> *   self*
> *and the wounds to the soul take a long, long time, only*
> *   time can help*
> *and patience, and a certain difficult repentance*
> *long, difficult repentance, realization of life's mistake, and*
> *   the freeing oneself*
> *from the endless repetition of the mistake*
> *which mankind at large has chosen to sanctify.*
> *   —"Healing," D.H. Lawrence*

Soul-loss, with its subsequent retrieval, has consistently and universally been an integral aspect of much indigenous shamanism. Archetypal psychologist Carl Jung, often called a modern shaman, regarded the loss of soul as one of the primary causes of the social upheaval and spiritual chaos of our times.

Carl Jung once commented, "There is no way out but through." This is a mantra for the Wounded Healers of today. The only way to embrace the light of dawn is to fully enter the dark unconscious of the night. The closing of the Piscean Age provides us with a vast vocabulary of healing technologies which we can wear like a tool belt for our transformations.

Past Life Therapy, birth trauma work, and early childhood up-bringing can paint the picture of the 'psychodynamics' at play—demonstrating the matrix of interconnection between our existential situation and previous soul-imprints. A skilled shaman, breathworker, or regression therapist can support the journey into recovering fragments of the soul in the return to wholeness. Modalities of breathwork, such as Rebirthing and Transformational Breathwork, apply affirmations as alchemical instruments which shift the old storylines of defeat and trauma, into inspired narratives of purpose, acceptance, and empowerment.

Beyond the Role

We often get stuck in defining ourselves in a limited fashion, as one of the characters in our narratives. In alchemy, this development stage is called the "Lesser Coniunctio," where we identify completely with one archetype, or our shadow, or our wound, or the masculine or feminine projection, the aenima or animus.

We arrive at a situation of 'false identification,' whereby the "messenger who can't deliver the message" limits his self-definition to being 'the messenger.' Naturally there are those that must receive the message, and if it can't be delivered then the messenger will either feel himself to be a failure and/or will feel victimized in the lack of ability to deliver the message.

But if 'the messenger' recognizes his vocation as a *role* to play in this incarnation, but not the *essence* of his identity, then he can transcend victimization and concepts of failure. Only the ego perceives lack and failure, and so only the ego suffers, but the ego is an impermanent hungry ghost, one that haunts, and one that perpetually wants. So the territorial ego, stuck in the reactive defensiveness and battlegrounds of the Will chakra, must choose to unite and reconcile in its ascended movement to the Heart charka.

For all healing occurs in the open and forgiving heart, the domain where Oneness can truly be realized. In the open heart, the self can at last recognize its inseparable and eternal nature. In alchemy this is the Philosopher's Stone, the Greater Coniunctio known as the goal of the entire Alchemical Opus.

What we must fully experience at the close of the Piscean Age is that the only thing which can truly save us is an authentic experience of our essential unity. The important irony to grasp is that *what seeks salvation dissolves away in the Unity experience.*

The realization becomes that there was never a separate, wounded self to begin with. As the Buddhists teach, there is no enlightenment to attain, for there is no self to attain it. This is the essential teaching on *sunyata*, or emptiness.

In Vedantic Indian philosophy, the concept of *neti, neti*—not this, not that—relates to emptiness. You are not any of the labels, definitions, or roles that you play. All of those are masks and costumes, shifting from one life to the next. You are at your essence the Absolute, the primal and preceding Alpha point of creation and eventual Omega point of all evolution.

A Course in Miracles affirms that the incarnate soul cannot be lacking and is consistently guided if open to receiving the message.

> *I am here only to be truly helpful.*
> *I am here to represent Him Who sent me.*
> *I do not have to worry about what to say or what to do,*
>   *because He Who sent me will direct me.*
> *I am content to be wherever He wishes, knowing He goes*
>   *there with me.*
> *I will be healed as I let Him teach me to heal.*

This statement reminds us that faith is required for personal revelation to occur, a fundamental concept to the early, mystical Christians, who called themselves Gnostics. Graham Hancock reminds us that they:

...believed that salvation was to be attained through a special sort of "knowledge of the true nature of things" that could not be taught but only revealed directly to the initiate. They also believed, like the Jivaro of Ecuador, that this material world in which we live is essentially an illusion in which the soul is trapped, and that the only way for us to see reality is to enter the visionary state.

Ultimately, the Gnostic or mystical experience unveils a truth which the visionary state teaches, a truth which will continue to sprout during the emerging Aquarian Age—that the individual self is the ultimate creator, and must serve the collective. Thus, the Shamanic Artist, the direct experiencer of the creative forces, becomes the voice of the next Great Age.

Pioneers in Psychic Exploration

One of the reasons it appears that the Aquarian age is rapidly emerging over planet earth in the 2010's and 2020's is because of the implications of an alpha and omega point occurring in two of the transpersonal planets: Uranus and Neptune.

Just as the 2012 end date of the Mayan calendar culminates, Neptune moves into his home sign of Pisces, the last sign of the zodiac, where he will remain until 2024. Simultaneously, Uranus enters Aries, the first sign of the zodiac, where he will stay through 2018.

No sign of the zodiac, and no planetary force of consciousness symbolize altered states of consciousness more than Pisces and Neptune. Thus, under Neptune in Pisces, the mystical experience will no longer be the domain of the few. There will continue to be increasing opportunities and desires for consciousness exploration and adjustment through pharmaceuticals, psychedelics, meditation, and other techniques of altering one's awareness. The field will continue to blur into a hypersurreal mirage, where waking, dream-

Psila MerKaBa (2006)

ing, virtual environments, and bardo states flow seamlessly as tides of the shifting self-perception.

What makes this more intriguing is that Uranus in Aries suggest the empowerment of the individual, and the daring leap into the adventure of evolution. This will increase the passion and will to push past our known versions of reality, both in the collective metanarrative and also in our personal sense of what an individual can achieve.

Both Pisces and Aries have a quality of the inner guidance system. For Pisces, we receive a vision, an intuitive download. At any moment, we can tap into the field of consciousness as a whole.

With Uranus in Aries, we feel the fire in the belly stir us, the hunch that catalyzes us, the instinctive call to action, the impulse we must follow.

And Neptune in Pisces represents the willingness to open and experience the unified field, and all of its manifold expressions, such as the idea that space is actually not a vacuum at all, but in fact a plenum—a fullness overflowing with accessible energy.

Likely, the paradigm will move into a further acceptance that, as mystics and Eastern religions have taught us, we are all indeed One, from the microcosmic quark particle to the macrocosmic and multi-dimensional soul.

This will likely also occur with the return to our mythical roots, for Pisces is the sign of myth and story. There will be new discoveries in our origin points as a species, most likely revealing our connections to other intelligent beings throughout the galaxies. These findings will force us to rewrite our creation myths and compose a new narrative which empowers humanity as one part of a wider field of co-existing spiritual realities.

There is a deep dive into Great Mystery with these planetary transits. Neptune in Pisces occurred during the great age of oceanic exploration and And Uranus in Aries is consistently a restless, experimental, and culturally and scientifically exciting cycle of new discoveries.

And importantly, Aries rules the head, and by extension the brain. Uranus is the planet of innovation and inventive thinking. It shocks us into the future. Thus, Uranus in Aries will invite more and more pioneers in the Piscean fields of the psyche and consciousness studies, and the role the brain plays as a receiver or antennae for consciousness. Those braving the cutting edge in these fields will ask what actually occurs in the brain as we dream, meditate, journey on psychedelics, etc. What chemicals are involved in what visionary experiences and what parallels can be found? We are now literally mapping the psyche: the cartography of the dreamspace, the experience of dying, of what occurs after we die, the womb state, our past lives, and the shamanic and visionary journey. Likewise, the "many-worlds" theory of physics, whereby each decision you make creates another universe and another and another, as overwhelming to consider as it may be, is becoming the most accepted theory on the nature of reality.

All of this combines to open into the new Aquarian paradigm, where the individual self becomes aware of its multidimensional nature as an energetic being, pulsing its vibrations across different fields of perception, some where time and space do not even exist.

To fully grasp this understanding of what it means to be human requires the Aquarian urge to synthesize information and ideas so that more rapid evolution can occur. Thus, we will continue to see movements towards more integral conferences, where all fields of study can merge together. In these open-minded, inspiring environments, all geniuses and experts can apply their Aquarian humanitarian efforts to reach towards the universal liberation of the earth and her species into a more refined and cosmic vibration.

Leo-Aquarian Artistry: One For All

The old way—that Virgo shadow-corpse—which we must transfigure, has a lot of reinforcement. The old paradigm tended to smile with approval when you talked in guilt and victim consciousness.

But the new paradigm demands personal response-ability for everything I experience. This is the essence of Leo, the polarity of the emerging Aquarian age. Everything that happens to me I ask for. I am creating all of it—this situation, this experience, this relationship—for my highest purpose.

During the Piscean Age, we have delegated our decisions, our feelings, and our spiritual truths to others, whether they be our bosses, police officers, educational institutions, religions, or governments, giving our authority and freedom away.

This occurred due to the Piscean need for faith of something outside of itself, and then the subsequent projection of salvation and authority towards that person, ideal, or institution. But the Aquarian Water Bearers must author their own lives. They must be the accountable carriers of their own consciousness, not fantasizing their redemption or self-understanding on an authority outside of themselves.

The evolutionary imperative is what drives Aquarius. Thus,

Aquarian motives are founded on constantly revolutionizing the present moment. In this, there is little time for personal wounds, shadow-triggers, and blame to run the show. For Aquarius, it is always a question of the appropriate use of creative energy. The pillars of the emerging zeitgeist will be humanitarian, group efforts and technological advancements which assist the realization of equal opportunities and maximized personal freedom for all people.

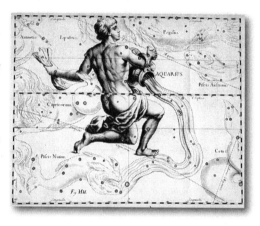

And as a microcosm of the macrocosmic creator, the ways in which we can best offer our unique gifts to the Aquarian collective is to approach life from a more experimental, experiential, and adaptive modality, which does not let the king-ego, the shadow of the cowardly lion Leo, manipulate a situation.

Under Aquarius, we must recognize the gifts that we come to share. The symbol for Aquarius appears as two waves of energy—vital, electricified waters of life.

Thus, the only real knowledge I can have is recognition and honoring of the play of energetic patterns within me, the archetypal forces that demonstrate my unique gifts and offerings to liberate humanity. Astrology, Human Design, Yoga and other systems of self awareness help awaken the creative responsibility which naturally blossoms under these languages of self-discovery

Just like the Pisces-Virgo polarity, in order to inaugurate the Aquarian age, we must beware the shadow polarity of Leo—egocentrism, the conceited artist, the irresponsible child, the self righteous drama queen, the arrogant dictator. We must instead sip the Leo medicine—unconditional creativity, the generous and open heart, the spontaneous and playful child, the artist who serves humanity.

To do this, we must get out of the way enough to allow ourselves to become the most appropriate channel for service at a particular time. My duty as creator, is to respond to the needs of the community in an act of selfless service.

 The archetype of the Wounded Healer is the integrated Pisces-Virgo, while the archetype of the Shamanic Artist is the integrated Aquarius-Leo. Because our lives comprise the peak centuries of transition between the Ages, we now merge the Wounded Healer and Shamanic Artist into a single archetype. This is the essence of the Shamanic Hero pulsing within each one of us, the light of a New Sun radiating from our crystalline hearts.

Infinitree (2007)

PART 2

CHIRON:
Myth and Medicine
of the Wounded Healer

CHAPTER 2

Peering Through the Window
of Galactic Alignment

The 13th Constellation: A cultural phenomena invoking the Wounded Healer

In January of 2011, an announcement by the Minnesota Planetarium Society spread like a virus through the web, flooding astrologer's inboxes. It suggested that the sun actually moves through a thirteenth sign of the zodiac and that this would shift everyone's astrology Sun signs.

Naturally, a panic ensued and people started questioning the validity of their Sun signs. It is true that the Sun actually moves through a 13th constellation. But astrologers from all traditions have been aware of this for millenia.

What was forgotten amidst the hoopla of this popular story was the significance of the 13th constellation. It is called Ophiuchus, or in the ancient world Serpentarius the Serpent Bearer. The most important fact is that the Serpent Bearer constellation is the celestial representation of the Greek god of healing, Asclepius.

Ophiuchus is located between the probing psychologist of Scorpio and the inspiring philosopher, Sagittarius. It is Asclepius, the divine healer within us, who must bridge the penetrating depth of the Scorpionic underworld with the Sagittarian pilgrim's quest for spiritual truth.

All three constellations are located at the Galactic Center, with Scorpio's tail pointing to it, the Sagittarian arrow aimed at, and the celestial shaman Ophiuchus' foot stomping down upon it. The Galactic Center is the black hole source for all stars and life in this galaxy. It is also the primary component of the prophetic and transformational Mayan calendar 2012 end date, signifying the alignment of the Galactic Center with the December Solstice Sun and the Earth.

Asclepius is truly a shamanic archetype, an energy collectively being remembered and evolved in today's shapeshifting world. It is my feeling that the 13th constellation arose in our collective consciousness in order to invoke a very special archetype seeking integration now in the transformation of consciousness occurring across this planet—that archetype is the Wounded Healer, the subject of this book. Asclepius was taught by Chiron—a wise centaur, a tireless mentor, and the template for the Wounded Healer, and by extension, the Shamanic Artists of today.

Mayan Prophecy and the Alignment Window

Hundreds of books have been released on the topic of the 2012 end date of the Mayan long-count calendar. They speak of a unique astronomical event—an alignment of the winter solstice Sun, the Earth, and the Galactic Center. This alignment has caused many researchers to formulate diverse and intriguing theories about collective consciousness at this apex moment. Although we have a sense of massive sociocultural and technological shifts occurring at this time, these studies have often lacked an essential astronomical fact which opens the door to the emergence of the Wounded Healer mythology as a significant expression of this powerful alignment.

In his book *Galactic Alignment*, eminent Mayan and 2012 scholar John Major Jenkins communicates an essential, but often ignored astronomical observation regarding the alignment of the December Solstice Sun, the Earth, and the Galactic Center.

Early on in my research, I recognized that the solstice-galaxy alignment would occur around 1998 or 1999. This was based on precise astronomical concepts (e.g., galactic equator and solstice colure) and a rough es-

timate I made with EZCosmos astronomy software, confirmed by the calculations of European astronomer Jean Meeus and the U.S. Naval Observatory...[The] fourteen year error between 1998 and 2012 amounts to less than one-fifth of a degree...The Sun itself is one-half a degree wide, so an alignment zone between 1980 and 2016 must be allowed, thus embracing the 2012 end-date.

Given this information, we should study what transpired imme-diately surrounding the opening window of solstice-galaxy align-ment around 1980, as well as the closing window, 2016, for insight into the experiential, embodied expressions of this prophesied alignment.

We will begin with the closing of the Galactic Alignment window and then return to its beginning.

Tikal Hinab Ku: The Shaman's Stairway (2006)

CHAPTER 3

The Uranus-Pluto Square:
Catharsis, Cacophony, and Creativity

The whirlwinds of revolt will continue to shake the foundations of our nation until the bright day of justice emerges....Again and again we must rise to the majestic heights of meeting physical force with soul force.

—Martin Luther King Jr.

From 2010 to 2016, the planets Uranus and Pluto face off in a tense, dynamic square. All coinciding world events should be viewed under the umbrella of this catalytic and revolutionary merger of two archetypal behemoths—Uranus and Pluto, who will be exactly squaring an unprecedented seven times in four years. The square is an aspect of friction, tension, and dynamic change.

In a sense, the first 5 years of the 2010s, each individual and all aspects of culture and social structure are being pummeled, remolded, and transfigured by the relentless Uranus-Pluto force.

With this planetary configuration, we can think of the enduring impact of the 1960's on the succeeding decades, for this was the last time these giant forces impacted planet earth. In a similar way, the energies, ideas, and movements of the 2010's will ripple out far into the future, especially as this Uranus-Pluto square correlates exactly to the close of the alignment between the galactic center, the earth, and the winter solstice sun.

In 2010, Uranus began a new phase of its evolution in our collective psyche, as it moved from the last sign of the zodiac, Pisces, to the first sign Aries. Simultaneously, Uranus began its intense and powerful square to Pluto.

Uranus is the great awakener, the paradigm shifter, the revolutionary genius—a rebellious Prometheus stealing fire from the gods to liberate humanity. Pluto is Lord of the Underworld, the harbinger of cathartic and profound evolutionary shift, through relentless transformation, regeneration, death, and rebirth.

The two in the dynamic square aspect promise a totalizing effect that catalyzes a radical shapeshift in all aspects of culture, stripping us of what is no longer essential and what has outlived its usefulness. Consistent themes of Uranus-Pluto as expressed in Richard Tarnas' thorough and fascinating research into planetary cycles, *Cosmos and Psyche*, include:

- Widespread radical social and political change
- Often destructive upheaval
- Massive empowerment of revolutionary and rebellious impulse
- Intensified artistic and intellectual creativity
- Extremely rapid technological advancement
- An underlying spirit of restless experiment
- Drive for innovation
- Urge for freedom resulting in a revolt against oppression
- Embrace of radical political philosophies
- Intensified collective will to bring forth a new world
- Massive demographic shifts
- Fervent, often violent intensity
- Excitement of moving rapidly toward new horizons

2011's worldwide revolutions, including Egypt, the Middle East, and the Occupy Wall St. and global Occupy movements, all reflect the volcanic intensity and transformational potency of the Uranus-Pluto square.

It will be up to the artists, healers, and lightworkers to vibrate at a frequency so high as to magnetize others in our collective ascension to a more enlightened species.

Every thought, vision, and action is a step towards this. Every gathering, every intimate encounter, every conversation is an opportunity to answer the evolutionary call.

Uranus in Aries: Call to Freedom

Uranus steps boldly into Aries beginning April of 2011—the warrior, freedom-fighter, pioneer, and competitive reactionary—during its square to Pluto in Capricorn. Whatever slumber some of us have been in, fascinated with the distractions of our gizmos, keeping up with our online profiles, or drowning in the dramas of the Piscean seas, Uranus in Aries will now demand that we manifest those Piscean dreams in the world, as he asserts a forceful call to action and a thrust towards greater freedom.

The catalyzing fires of this transit have been demonstrated on the geophysical plane, for instance during Uranus's first ferocious months in Aries in summer 2010. This included the summer volcano over Iceland. Worldwide, 2010's summer was often found to be the hottest on record. And in 2011, according to climatecentral. org, "June, July, and August saw more warm temperature records tied or broken than any other summer in the past decade: more than 26,500 record warm temperatures were set across the nation. The blazing storm of Uranus in Aries was also depicted in Summer 2011's nuclear disaster in Japan.

The blood, like the earth, literally boils under Uranus in Aries, which compels all of us to forge into territory never thought possible before. The risk-taker dares us to not only think, but ACT outside of the box. Keep talking about that sustainable community or retreat center you want to build, or class you want to teach or education you're dying to know? It's time to experiment, as Aries learns by doing. The acceleration of the 2010's cannot be overestimated. Our ability to remain adaptable is a major test and new knowledge is streaming in. As we chase the flame of our evolution, we may find ourselves taking two steps forward and one step back, and we have to learn to accept and adjust.

With Uranus in Aries square Pluto in Capricorn, the sudden explosion of changes in our lives demands that we at last embrace the lessons of impermanence. To honor impermanence is to give each moment its gratitude. The Latin phrase Carpe Diem, or "seize the day" is the mantra of Uranus in Aries. Thus, the decade of the 2010's will be spurned forward by entrepreneurial spirit, daring each one of us to find our original voice, carve our unique niche, spark inspiration in others, and as Joseph Campbell advised, "Follow your bliss."

We repeatedly here the phrase, "We are the ones we have been waiting for." But, it is Gandhi's phrase "Be the change you want to see in the world," which then motivates us to access the avatar—the chosen one—within. To "be the change" is not a passive state of being, but an active and passionate leadership by example.

Gandhi's salt march occurred during Uranus' transit in Aries in 1930, when it last squared Pluto. Martin Luther King Jr. was born during this same transit, just two years before the salt march. King led his own protest march during the following connection between Uranus and Pluto throughout the decade of the 60's.

Both King and Gandhi preached and practiced non-violent resistance, influenced by another Uranus in Aries and Uranus-Pluto figure: Henry David Thoreau, whose *On Civil Disobedience* stated: "That government is best which governs not at all and when men are prepared for it, that will be the kind of government which they will have. Government is at best but an expedient; but most governments are usually, and all governments are sometimes, inexpedient."

Pluto in Capricorn: Unveil to Evolve

The inexpediency and irrelevancy of governments today has ignited the civil unrest erupting all over the world as citizens recognize their governments as puppets to corporations who only desire power and only think of people as sources of money.

In essence, Pluto in Capricorn unveils the unconscious forces we have all participated in, as related to the structures of the world.

Dorje L.A (2006)

These Capricornian systems include governments, corporations, banking and money, resource management. Through a process of revealing the ugly, hidden truth of these areas, Pluto destroys through decay all of that which is no longer evolutionary in the

Capricorn archetype. Necessarily, this will give rise to that which is *sustainable*, a concept which drives Capricornian ethics. This helps us to understand the resurgence in the 2010's of native and indigenous traditions, ceremonies, and medicines, all of which invoke the healthiest expression of Capricorn—the wise elder. Each one of us is being challenged to become accountable for our actions, and respond with integrity and sincerity to life's challenges, as a chief or a leader required to make tough decisions which will affect the whole.

We should ask how can we take the militant fervor we feel within and cultivate courage in the face of our personal and collective fears. As MLK Jr. stated, "Militancy means persistence, to be demanding, to be insistent..."

How do we update the revolutionary fervor of the 1960's (last Uranus-Pluto alignment) and avoid the destructive, violent potential of previous cycles, such as the French and American Revolution?

Spiritual and artistic rebellions are at the core of inspiring mass change through example. Yoga and meditation flash mobs on state capitols, such as January 2011's Austin, Texas flash mob, as well as the incorporation of music, live painting, and art, into a protest environment, inspire the creative pulse and the tribal bonds which unite humanity.

At the close of Galactic Alignment, humanity worldwide is now insisting on a new system altogether, inspired by visions such as the resource-based economy, as described in *Zeitgeist Addendum* and *Zeitgeist Moving Forward*. The Zeitgeist movement (zeitgeistmovie.com) is a worldwide revolution occurring with planetary activists everywhere, supporting many ideas espoused by the Venus Project, especially the implementation of an economy that moves beyond money and its capitalist, consumerist model of competition and scarcity, choosing instead equal distribution of the earth's naturally abundant and renewable resources.

It is important for us to consider here the Hindu deity of Shiva, for Shiva is both creator and destroyer. We must allow the natural dissolving of those outdated and toxic structures, so that a cleansed womb may be sculpted out of which humanity's fertile creative potential may erupt into its luminous existence.

For this shift is not an overnight process, but begins to transmute slowly as more of us look to our local communities for support, including neighborhood gardens and community sponsored agriculture. These, coupled with permacultural practices and the implementation of worldwide educational ecovillages, support individuals accessing their personal power and responsibility—acute expressions of the archetypes of both Aries and Capricorn.

Living environments and educational centers which support holistic experiences of growth—artistically, ecologically, and in personal healing practices—will continue to proliferate as more of us become aware of our creative potential at the close of Galactic Alignment. At the end of one age, this foundation will birth the "New Sun," of which the Mayan prophecies speak.

In addition, the cultural innovations consistent during Uranus-Pluto cycles will accelerate and inspire us to push the limits of our imagination. We can think of the new forms of art, music, and ideas that proliferated during the psychedelic fervor of the 1960's, during the last Uranus-Pluto conjunction. Yet now, psychedelic conferences and scientific studies on the effects of psychedelics, meditation, and other altered states of consciousness are happening worldwide, as medical marijuana continues to be integrated and accepted by cities and states across the United States.

What differentiates this Uranus-Pluto cycle from the chaotic conjunction of the 1960's is that the square requires more solid ground, more stable roots under its experimental excitement. Thus, the wild "Electric Kool-Aid" LSD reveries of the 60's give way to plant medicine ceremonies, often incorporating native shamans, or tools and techniques from global wisdom traditions.

The "free love" of the 60's now invites us into deeper practices of evolutionary intimacy, such as heart-opening pujas and eyegazing of White Tantra, the yogic alchemy of Red Tantra between two beloveds. These also include cuddle parties and play parties—environments which support arousal and experimentation with many people within a community container—or commitment ceremonies such as handfastings and handpartings, which allow stable support for couples for sacred periods of time, such as from solstice to solstice, or for a year and a day.

The jam and rock music and the abstract expressionist art of the 60's or the dada surrealists of the 1930s Uranus-Pluto square now upgrades into the unlimited potential of the internet artist—a collage dj, able to mix video and sound from any time period, any genre, and culture, into a glorious puzzle of collective consciousness.

Thus, under Uranus in Aries square Pluto in Capricorn, the political revolutions are founded upon the revelations within the individual soul. For, the closing of the Galactic Alignment window has also included the Chiron-Neptune conjunction of 2009-2011. This merger of cosmic forces has helped to blossom the Wounded Healer archetype, who has united with the Shamanic Artist within each one of us, activating our inner mentor often through a painful experience which revealed areas of core wounding.

The unveiling of our unconscious wounds has helped to promote the personal healing journey, invoking the teacher and creative within, but only to the extent that we continue to will our trance-formations. For, like a zen master slapping our slacked posture, Chiron continuously modifies and tweaks our consciousness, demonstrating what is lacking, the skills undeveloped, the lessons not integrated, the unhealthy practices. Chiron whispers at us from within, that voice that says, "If I don't do my yoga today, then I'm going to be unbalanced for the rest of my day," or "I need to move this negative emotion through some breathwork or dance or a medicine ceremony." The connection with Neptune has helped unify this movement to return to the innocence of our spiritual essence. We are constantly reminded of this potential for re-union from the healers and artists within and around us. We can gain support from our imaginations and the endless beauty and majesty of the spirit-world

Healing is an active verb, a constant process, a total commitment. We try to balance ourselves on the Middle Way path to the cessation of suffering. With our meditation, with our spiritual practice, with archetypal languages of soul, and by crafting the artistic channel, prying our third eyes open wide, this healing unfolds from ever wider circles of holistic awareness and integral wisdom. Our wounds are experienced with less suffering and *perceived* as a necessary teacher and instructive guide for our spiritual service to the beings of this precious earth.

CHAPTER 4

The Centaur of the Galaxy

The celestial body Chiron orbits from within Saturn and beyond Uranus, the traditional and modern rulers of Aquarius, suggesting that Chiron, the "Wounded Healer," is the most essential archetypal force bridging the Piscean and Aquarian ages. In addition, Chiron travels from the sign of Aquarius (2004-2011) to Pisces (2011-2018) immediately surrounding the 2012 end date of the Mayan calendar, and the 2016 close of the alignment window. This once again demonstrates Chiron's fundamental role as an agent in the shift of the ages at this time of crisis and revelation.

We have just examined the world of today and the decade of the 2010s, the closing of the Galactic Alignment window. But what occurred around 1980, the opening of the Galactic portal? Most notably, for astrologers and astronomers alike, a planetoid named Chiron was discovered—part planet, part asteroid, whose mythology has been guiding the major planetary transformations since its discovery

The discovery of a heavenly body awakens within us an archetype, a primal pattern of cosmic energy. What we see above us reflects a fundamental psychic reality within, as the Hermeticists, Gnostics, alchemists, and sages have always taught, "As above, so below." In addition, the horoscope for the discovery moment of any planet reflects the essential nature and fundamental meaning of the planetary archetype. Before studying the discovery chart for Chiron, let us first examine the discovery of the three Outer Planets to elucidate this point.

Uranus - Uranus was discovered in 1781 by William Herschel as the first planet ever discovered through an instrument, the telescope. The discovery occurred during some of the most volatile revolutionary times in history, including the French and American Revolution. Appropriately, the archetype of Uranus reflects all desires for freedom, rebellion, and sudden, epiphanous moments of awakening, including scientific and technological innovation, which manifested at this time in the Industrial Revolution.

Neptune - Neptune was discovered in 1848, amidst the confusion it often symbolizes, as there could have been many possible discoverers. Neptune is associated with collectivist ideals and spiritual longings and in 1848, the Communist manifesto was written amidst widespread people's revolutions in Europe. Neptune rules illusion, the imagination, and the occult, including other dimensions of consciousness. The first cameras and the popularization of photography appeared around Neptune's discovery. Anaesthetics began to be employed in medicine, hypnotism began to be applied and more accepted, and Spiritualism spread as a religious movement, highly influenced by its seances.

Pluto - Pluto rules all realms of devastating power, control, transformation, death, regeneration and evolutionary necessity. Appropriately, Pluto was discovered in 1930 during the rise of totalitarian and dictatorial regimes in the buildup to the Second World War. Atomic energy developed out of the discovery of nuclear fission shortly after Pluto's discovery. In addition, Pluto, whose name means "wealth," was also discovered when the wealth of the world was stripped away during the Great Depression.

Chiron was discovered by Charles T. Kowal on November 1st, 1977 around 10 am in Pasadena, California. To understand more of Chiron's significance, we should first explore how the horoscope for the discovery date reflects some of the major archetypal motifs of Chiron, both in myth and in function for personal and collective experience. We should also study some of the major cultural events in the world near the discovery date—the archetype's moment of impact on our consciousness.

Bridge and Hybrid: Clues to Chiron's Meaning in the Discovery chart

Significantly, when Chiron was discovered, the Galactic Center was on the horizon. In our personal charts, we call this horizon point the Ascendant, or Rising Sign, one of the most important points in an individual or country's birth chart. The Ascendant is our outer mask and persona, our disposition and behavior emanating the energy which others receive from us. It describes much about our role in the world. To have the Galactic Center on the Ascendant during the discovery moment of Chiron suggests that the myths and science associated with the Galactic Center reflect much of Chiron's poignant message to us.

Each degree of the zodiac has a symbol associated with it, similar to the I CHING. These 360 Sabian symbols can act as a right brain, intuitive tool for understanding planetary positions in the horoscope or in this case, the role Chiron may be playing in the collective. The Sabian Symbol for Chiron's discovery degree is *"The sculptor's vision is taking form under his hands."* This powerful symbol makes us ask, who is the sculptor? Who is the architect of this glorious grand design? It is a fitting symbol for the area of our skies which gave birth to all the known stars in our galaxy.

It is important as well because Chiron's name means "hand," an extension of our creative intelligence and artistic motivations.

In 2010, the Galactic center shifted from the 27th to the 28th degree of Sagittarius. This occurs only every 72 years. Because of 2010's close vicinity to the 2012 end date of the Mayan calendar, the symbol of this degree may also elucidate the meaning of this prophecy. 28 degrees Sagittarius is *"A bridge linking the earthly with the celestial."*

This symbol for Chiron's Ascendant seems to suggest that Chiron's outer role is to instruct us how to link the earthy with the celestial, the wisdom once again of the Hermetic maxim "As Above So Below." Chiron has been called the "rainbow bridge" by author and astrologer Barbara Hand Clow because its symbol binds the socializing forces of Jupiter and Saturn, which connect us with social duty, roles, and occupation, with the transpersonalizing forces of the outer planets, Uranus, Neptune, and Pluto, which we discussed above.

The only heavenly body that crosses the orbit of Saturn and Uranus is Chiron. Thus Chiron bridges the "known and unknown" since Saturn is the last planet seen with the naked eye, and Uranus, the first to be discovered through the technology of a telescope.

Chiron, like the shamanic-artist within us, must consistently tweak, adapt, and shapeshift energy in order to translate to the third dimension the more liberating, visionary, cathartic, and evolutionary urges of the outer planets.

As we shall see, Chiron rules both alternative energies and alternative healing, for he is grounding the technologies of the future, helping to implement the Uranian paradigm shifts into the Saturnian structures of society.

Mythically, this position in the heavens for Chiron is also very important because Chiron's ancestral lineage includes both Saturn (Chronos), his father, and Uranus (Ouranos) his grandfather. Because Chiron orbits between these two planets, he is symbolically linking our conscious origins—our biological family and the world we know (Saturn) with our personal subconscious—the traits, tendencies, stories, and even wounds we inherit from our ancestors.

Like Chiron, we are all children of an emerging Age. Thus, Chiron's position between his father and his grandfather reflects the need for ancestor healing and intergenerational dialogue in our adaptation to a new energetic vibration. We shall explore this more below.

Chiron has been called a "maverick" because of his obscure orbit. In fact, Chiron's orbit and composition so defied known astronomical parameters that astronomers had to create a new label for Chiron—a planetoid—and a new category of heavenly objects which they appropriately called "the centaurs." These bodies behave in a dual way, like both asteroids and comets. Thus the mythical centaurs of ancient Greece—half-human, half-horse—were an appropriate reference.

Astrologers and astronomers co-operated in the naming process for several of the Centaurs, including Chiron, and this is the first time in recorded history that this collaboration has transpired. This fact reflects Centaur themes: the "bridging" of the scientific and the intuitive, the rational and inspirational, just as the half-horse, half-human image of the centaur brings together disparate opposites, and challenges us to integrate that which seems alien.

The Centaurs are minor planets which have very elliptical orbits, causing them to appear to speed through certain signs, while taking much longer in other areas of the zodiac. For instance, Chiron spends about eight years in Aquarius and Pisces, but only two years in Virgo and Libra. Although erratic through the signs, Chiron completes its journey around the Sun, returning to its natal place, consistently after fifty years. During this major life initiation, the Chiron Return, you will be required to confront, transform, and heal your wounds in order to serve the collective. This is an initiation when the higher octave of your life purpose can be realized. The Chiron return is covered in more detail in the closing section of this book.

As we begin to understand the association between the Wounded Healer and Shamanic Artist with Chiron, we can feel why it is so important that the Centaurs defy categorization, a necessary prerequisite in the art of translation. This maverick, world-bridging energy may be exactly why Chiron is the key linking us between the Piscean and Aquarian ages. In fact, Chiron's symbol looks exactly like a key.

Chiron's Cultural Significance

To understand the character and meaning of an archetype in the collective consciousness, we must study the period surrounding its discovery. What ideas, images, trends, and fashions emerged in the collective consciousness?

1977, the year of Chiron's discovery, was the Year of the Serpent according to Chinese Astrology. As Chiron's archetype began to disseminate into collective awareness, we progressed into 1978, the Year of the Horse. More than any other animals, Chiron relates to the transformative and regenerative shadow-work of snake symbology and of course, as a centaur, to the horse.

The year of the Serpent has had profound ramifications in recent history:

1989 - The Fall of the Berlin Wall. The two separate serpents reunite and the Western and Eastern worlds begin to change costumes. Capitalism spreads as a driving mythos into Eastern Europe and Asia, while Eastern spirituality such as Yoga begins to spread its popularity into the Americas.

2001 - The attack on the Twin Towers. The unintegrated serpent spits its poisonous venom as the dark unconscious ruptures out onto the planet.

2013 - The first full year after the 2012 prophecies. The world is "occupied" by millions of people in protest as dictatorial regimes are being dismantled and national economies dissolve away. The technowizard pulses through the palm of our hand, as we all step further into becoming Homo-Roboticus. The Feathered Serpent of Binary Light—the shamanic artist emerges as the hero of the next Solar Age.

Film

In film, the great heroic myth of our time, *Star Wars*, was released during 1977's Year of the Serpent, becoming the highest grossing movie at the time. More importantly, Star Wars became the prototype of every science fiction film created thereafter. The entire genre of "science fiction" is an expression of the Chiron archetype, bridging fact and fantasy, the solid realms of the known and the liquid possibilities of the unknown.

On a deeper, archetypal level, *Star Wars* is our modern myth of shamanic initiation. The film introduced all of us to a pop-culture Chiron figure, Obi-Wan Kenobi—the mentor and guide to Luke

Skywalker. Obi-wan instructs Luke on the true nature of reality and the Force, just as contemporary Chiron figures—teaching yoga, chi kung, energy healing, and life-coaching. Also, the shamanic hero, Luke Skywalker's last name recalls the sabian symbol of 28 degrees Sagittarius—*a bridge linking the earthly to the celestial.*

In *The Empire Strikes Back*, Yoda, another Chiron figure, teaches Luke about the Wounded Healer archetype by training him to dance with his shadow and how to recognize and transmute the seduction of the Dark Side.

Chiron pries open our consciousness to perceptions never before accessed. In the bar scene on Tattoine, Star Wars introduced us to gangs of alien beings –very distinct species. This also includes R2D2 and C3PO, robotic intelligences. These characters offer clues to our future advancements and developments, from our status quo Saturnian reality paradigms, and into a Uranian galactic civilization of thousands of species. This accelerating future includes our reliance upon and merger with machine intelligences, a major theme of the emerging Aquarian Age.

Also, Chiron's Wounded Healer themes, which we discuss below, are very active in the Star Wars films, including the orphaned heroes (Luke and Leia) and the need to heal the ancestral lineage (Luke and Darth Vader).

Close Encounters of the Third Kind also achieved the same effect amidst Chiron's discovery. These films demonstrate repeated themes of the meetings between humanity and alien intelligence, directing us to turn our focus towards Chiron's invitation. This message is that we must continue to adapt the Earth and welcome our encounter with Aquarian motifs—the interaction with unparalleled technologies of both liberation and control, as well as meetings with extraterrestrial and interdimensional beings—the centaur spirit guiding the cyber-human in its hybrid becoming as both electronic and interstellar.

Books and Teachings

Fresh from his years of research with LSD psychotherapy and Holotropic breathwork, Stanislav Grof, with Buddhist and shamanic practitioner Joan Halifax, released one of his most important works, *The Human Encounter with Death*. This is also when Halifax deepened her work with shamans, and a few years later released her influential book, *Shaman, the Wounded Healer*.

Ken Wilber's first book, *A Spectrum of Consciousness,* appeared in 1977, the year of Chiron's discovery, and was a foundational component in supporting consciousness studies and in the development of transpersonal psychology. In *A Spectrum of Consciousness,* Wilber performed the role of the Chiron world-bridger, discussing, criticizing, and integrating many spiritual disciplines and philosophies from both Eastern and Western traditions.

The work addresses stages of consciousness development, leading towards an integral approach of mythology, psychology, religion, philosophy, anthropology, science, sociology, and prehistory. Wilber even refers to the stage of "centauric" consciousness, involving body-mind integration and an existential type of cognition.

In a similar vein, Fritjof Capra's *Tao of Physics,* released in 1975, pried open a new lens of perception throughout scientific and spiritual communities. The *Tao of Physics* was a pioneering exploration of Eastern Mysticism and modern physics, shifting the old paradigm separating science and religion. It became highly influential throughout the entire window of Galactic Alignment from 1980-2016, seeding the hundreds of books now written on spirituality and science.

Interestingly, it was through shamanic practices that Capra received many of his original insights. In the preface to his first edition, he writes that he was "helped on my way by 'power plants'" or psychedelics with the first experience "so overwhelming that I burst into tears, at the same time, not unlike Castaneda pouring out my impressions to a piece of paper."

Also in 1977, Robert Anton Wilson's seminal cult classic, *The*

Cosmic Trigger was released, a very significant study in the esoteric and occult world. It demonstrates the spiritual epiphanies which can be produced from attention to synchronicity .

As Barbara Hand Clow has eloquently written,

> *Chiron rules the synchronicity principle and the art of divination itself, because it explicitly focuses into Saturnian time higher dimensions ruled by Uranus, Neptune, and Pluto. The way the story unfolds is just as important as the story itself....Chiron rules the way, gate, or key to mastery, because it is the bridge to the outer planets. Once we have learned to use the outer planet energies, then we are capable of working with mastery. Mastery is the conscious evolution of self with magical forces"*

Teachings on personal mastery also disseminated into the world near Chiron's discovery, reflecting the wisdom of multi-dimensional consciousness. These include the popularity of Jane Robert's *Seth* teachings, Carlos Castaneda's *Don Juan* books, as well as *A Course in Miracles*, a profound correction in Christianity and a manual for shifting one's self perception to radical responsibility.

CHAPTER 5

Chiron: The Mentor in the Myth

Take your pain
and wrap your heartstrings around it.

Like tinsel on fire
slip the cello bow through
then entangle your shamanbones
in the dance
of catharsis
AlchemEyez
Uncover what you can no longer hide

Dissolve to coagulate
breakdown to breakthrough
you are re-membering you
together, whole, One

your pain, your gift
of the present tense
present
tense

Remember
the orphan
is found
by the god of light.

Who was Chiron and how does this archetypal energy fulfill the prophecies of a Neo-human who is bridging the Piscean and Aquarian ages—the Wounded Healer, the shamanic artist seeking the cure to the wounds of the physical, emotional, mental, and spiritual bodies?

Chiron is wounded in three primary ways, which each of us will feel woven within our own individual mythos. These are the qualities of feeling exiled, having a hybrid nature, and being chosen for a mission.

Exile: The Fortune of the Fates

"We are lived by Powers we pretend to understand"
—W.H. Auden

"When an inner situation is not made conscious, it appears outside as fate."
—Carl Jung

Chiron is a centaur. He is born out of an illicit affair between Saturn (Greek Chronos) and Philyra, a sea-nymph. The two of them turn into horses in order to not be caught, and they mate in this way, conceiving Chiron. He is a bastard child, **rejected** by his parents for being too ugly; thus, he becomes **orphaned**, and represents the **wounded and exiled** parts of ourselves.

The orphaned and rejected aspects of ourselves can create an overwhelming sense of victimization, a feeling that forces are conspiring against us. Under these circumstances, we often say, "It is my fate," in a way that disempowers us. But we cannot clearly understand the word "fate" until we excavate the root of the word. The Greek Fates are the arbiters of one's karma, which is a collection of our choices from previous lifetimes and from decisions we make with our guides before we incarnate.

According to the Vedic tradition, the three kinds of karma include Pralabd Karma, Kriyaman Karma, and Sinchit Karma. Pralabd Karma refers to an unalterable series of experiences an individual must deal with in this incarnation. Kriyaman Karma refers to the karma we are making in this lifetime, the effects of which we will have to face in future incarnations. Sinchit Karma refers to karma that we have accumulated from our thousands of lifetimes but which is not specifically active in this lifetime, for we could not possibly handle the psychic, physical, and emotional repercussions of so much energy in a single human body confined to third dimensional space and time.

Through our karma, **WE** choose our fate, and then our Fates command us to follow our own decree. Upon our decision to reincarnate we are given a *daimon*, a tutelary spirit, to assure we stay on our destined or fated path, fulfilling our Pralabd Karma.

The Decree and Design of the Daimon

Today, we speak in an often vague sense of spirit guides, but in the ancient Greek, Roman, Arabic, and Indian worlds, the awareness of the daimon was mainstream. This was especially true under Plato's cosmology, which influenced gnostics, alchemists, and sages for centuries following the great thinker's life.

Scholar and therapist Stephen Diamond describes how Plato referred to the great god of love, Eros, as "a daimon," and that Plato communicated the story of the *daimonion* of Socrates: the supposedly supernatural "voice" inside the head of Socrates, which spoke to him whenever he was about to make some mistaken decision.

Almost all esoteric religions and philosophical systems have a concept of the daimon. In the language of the Sufis, as extrapolated by esteemed scholar, Henri Corbin, the daimon was called the Man of Light, the "perfect nature." For the Zoroastrian Persians, it was called Daena. It was called variously, the Heavenly Twin, the Angel of Light, and Phos—a Greek word signifying that which emanates light.

Rumi often wrote of the daimon, whom he called, "The Friend."

If you can't do this work yourself, don't worry.
You don't even have to make a decision,
one way or another. The Friend, who knows
a lot more than you do, will bring difficulties
and grief, and sickness
                as medicine....

With this verse, Rumi suggests that life's wounding situations are in fact offerings from our higher selves, our daimons. Pride and worry, however, cloud the true purpose of life's turmoils. However, if we remain humble before the difficulties presented by the daimon, these great challenges will grant us the ability to empathize and heal.

Scholars such as Anthony Peake and Patrick Harpur have written extensively and profoundly on the subject of the daimon across cultures. In *The Daemon: A Guide to Your Extraordinary Secret Self*, Peake quotes Carl Jung, who referred to his daimon, Philemon, as no less than the source of his awareness of the objective psyche.

> *Philemon and other figures of my fantasies brought home to me the crucial insight that there are things in the psyche which I do not produce, but which produce themselves and have their own life....In my fantasies I held conversations with him, and he said things which I had not consciously thought. For I observed clearly that it was he who spoke, not I. He said I treated thoughts as if I generated them myself, but in his view thoughts were like animals in a forest, or people in a room, or birds in the air... It was he who taught me psychic objectivity.*

How does the daimon reveal itself to us? Through that prophetic voice inside your head, that entity in your vision, that mystic figure in your dreams, the fully composed song that channels through you, the hand who paints the esoteric symbols upon your canvas, the one who writes your poem, your novel, your guidebook for others—that inkling within. And what becomes most important in this recognition of The Inner Other is our welcoming embrace of this higher nature.

The awareness of the spirit guide daimon, assuring the realization of our Fate, has been seeping back into our culture with the strong presence of the emerging Wounded Healer archetype. One can look to the following powerful synchronicity in the world of film to understand the role of the daimon. The actor Matt Damon, whose name literally has the word 'daimon' in it, starred in two films in 2010 which explicitly demonstrate the presence of the higher self that links one to the transpersonal realms.

In *Hereafter*, Damon plays a psychic overwhelmed by the part of himself which has the capacity to read into the souls of people. He is afflicted by his own unwillingness to accept the vocation of healer, and in doing so, first heal himself. In *The Adjustment Bureau*, Damon's character is a politician who is followed by a bunch of suits called simply the Adjustment Bureau. The job of the Bureau's "caseworkers" is to ensure people's lives proceed as determined by "the plan."

The film was based on a story by Philip K. Dick, from whom many prophetic science fiction films, such as *Minority Report* and *Total Recall*, have been made. Dick wrote, "Each of us has a divine counterpart unfallen who can reach a hand down to us to awaken us. This other personality is the authentic waking self; the one we have now is asleep and minor."

In another striking similarity of names, (which, in an eerie but humorous way, seems to prove the existence of the daimons,) psychotherapist Stephen **Diamond's** riveting essay "The Psychology of Evil", describes the various meanings and history of the terms demon, daimon, devil, and evil.

> *The daimon was that divine, mediating spiritual power that impelled one's actions and determined one's des-*

The Hidden Captain (2005)

tiny. It was, in the judgment of most scholars, inborn and immortal, embodying all innate talents, tendencies (both positive and negative), and natural abilities. Indeed, one's daimon manifested as a sort of fateful 'soul'...

Thus, the daimon functions as both guide, navigator, and the voice of warning. The pre-destined presence of the daimon in our lives functions as the spiritual mechanism by which the karmic laws of third-dimensional density operate, helping us to accept that nothing is an accident. By cultivating our connection to our daimon, as the captain of our embodied vehicles, as the navigational higher self, we can begin to let go of our attempts to control or question our situation. Instead, the relationship can help us establish pillars of enduring trust in this moment to provide all the necessities of our spiritual growth.

In the teachings of the spirit of Oneness, channeled by Rasha,

To break the patterns of dependency upon the influence of others it is necessary to understand that the answers themselves do not matter at all. The act of seeking those answers is merely an exercise you have devised in order to guide yourself to the path that leads within. Ultimately, the life altering choices you have created to confound yourself fade into obscurity, along with the very crossroads that prompted them. And you emerge in a place of knowingness that the questions—and the answers—are unimportant. They are simply vehicles that deliver you to a place of unconditional trust in your own ability to derive a sense of inner directness in any circumstances.

This quote invites us to perceive those experiences of profound 'fatedness', as the acts of our guides directing us on our soul's path. The centaur Chiron understood the truth about the Fates, and the role of the daimons. Thus, he studied and mastered the science and art of astrology as a language reflecting our fate, thereby helping us fulfill our destiny. Our choice is where on the spectrum of consciousness we choose to act from, for we can act with ignorance and victimization or with acute awareness in the mission of fulfilling our chosen paths.

In a sense, the planets act as daimons. Referring to the original derivation of the term, we discover that dai-mon means "divider, provider, allotter" of fortune or destinies. The planets are these intermediary forces, allotting us a range of options, which are not infinite, but provide certain destined parameters of experience. They tether us to types of events, life situations, and relationships, and describe the impressions and reactions we have accumulated through lifetimes. In Vedic astrology, they are called "grahas," which means graspings, for the planets compel and magnetize our behaviors to fit the necessities of our karma.

For example, how have I learned to perceive faith, trust, and intuitive guidance (Jupiter's sign, house, aspect)? How do I perceive the need to discipline, work hard, and face challenge and frustration? (Saturn) What patterns have I built towards attracting and relating with others? (Venus) What flame simmers my will and desires? (Mars)

The Wounded Healer and Shamanic Artist who becomes aware of these orbiting patterns of behavior—these daimonic planetary intelligences—must transform herself from the sulking victim of these forces to the harmonic instrument in the Music of the Spheres. Realizing that one has composed the entire score of one's life, and that the daimon is conducting the orchestra of events, is a fundamental goal in awakening to a persistent acceptance, an attuned awareness, and a dedicated service to all beings.

We may argue that our ultimate spiritual goal is *nirvana*, which literally means "where the wind of karma does not blow." Thus, says the argument, we should not give much attention to our charts since we should transcend them. Yet, these planetary *sanskaras,* these soul attachments and tendencies, are impossible to transcend, since they describe the karmic accumulations over lifetimes, which, while we are in the body, hunt and haunt us. As the poet W.H. Auden said, "As well these persons who appear to us as our daimons make possible our modes of perception and our styles of participation in the reality of things."

We cannot help but to act out this karmic residue, but our goal is to utilize languages to help us navigate the quicksand terrain of ego desires and habitual patterns. Astrology has universally been recognized as a highly specific instrument for recognizing what Stephen Arroyo calls, "the past *creative use or misuse* of our powers." Thus, this cosmic, linguistic lens instructs the individual to his or her response-ability to life situations, while prying open the path for attuning oneself to the most universally positive expression of our spiritual duty, and thereby transmute our karma into our dharma, our true purpose.

Ancestral Healing

"We choose our joys and sorrows long before we experience them."
—*Khalil Gibran*

Our families of origin are an expression of our karmic necessity. Chiron chose a very unique fate: to be born of a father in Saturn and a grandfather in Uranus. Both of these gods destroyed or abandoned their children. Saturn-Chronos ate all his children, or neglected them, as in Chiron's case, and Uranus stuffed his children in the underworld of Tartarus until Saturn castrated him.

Like us, Chiron *chose his family and early childhood experiences for evolutionary lessons*. Without being abandoned, the orphan Chiron would not have been found by Apollo—god of light, the sun, medicine, music, and the source of poetic inspiration and prophecy. Apollo instructs Chiron in the arts of self-reliance, including healing, herbology, astrology, astronomy, archery, music, and spiritual disciplines. Chiron's education into becoming a master teacher and healer, offers us a profoundly simple, yet consistently challenging truth to accept: that our present and past conditions, including our family of origin, are necessary and essential in forging our unique spiritual gifts. Thus, Chiron teaches us how to cultivate practices of self-inquiry leading to enhanced self-awareness.

Chiron also heals his ancestral baggage by instructing the next generation. Because he was orphaned and a demi-god, Chiron could empathize with and instruct Asclepius, another demi-god orphan, who was given to Chiron via Asclepius' father Apollo. Thus, Chiron's own wounded story is offered back as guidance to his pupil. Although Asclepius and Chiron's other students were not his children, Chiron evolved the previous generations as he guided the next generation. In this way, Chiron performed what Rebirthing co-founder Sondra Ray calls, "detaching from the family mind."

It is almost as if we must *choose* to orphan ourselves from our family of origin, in order to fully reveal our true essence. By staying

Ancestree (2006)

sheltered within the confines of our role expectations, we lack the vaster perspective of the Exile.

In *Letting Go of the Person You Used to Be,* Lama Surya Das reflects this similar sentiment of releasing those overidentified aspects of ourselves, "My own experience is that finding the divine in our lives is usually more of a matter of subtraction than addition."

By developing this skill, Chiron ended the destructive lineage of Saturn and Uranus, breaking the fear of responsible parenting. The result of this alchemical act in Chiron—to transcend a state of self-pity and become instead a mentor—has resulted in nothing less than the lineage of the Wounded Healer, including the guides, coaches, teachers, doctors, nurses, and healers of today.

Hybrid Identity: Between the Wounded, the Wounder, and the Healer

"There are two of you doing these things; one that kills and one that loves."
"I don't know if I'm an animal or a god!"
"But you are both!"
        —*Francis Ford Coppola, Apocalypse Now*

Chiron's second wound involves an identity crisis: as a centaur, he is neither totally wild, nor totally civilized. He is a demi-god and a hybrid being and so reflects that struggle within us towards integration of our human, animal, divine, and in contemporary times, our machine natures.

Like shamans across cultures, Chiron must negotiate the worlds. He spends much of his time alone in his cave, communing with Spirit. Importantly, his solitude affords him the ability to develop his creative and healing gifts, which include the studies of music, astrology, astronomy, herbology, and weaponry. When he interacts with others, he is usually teaching or guiding them. Thus, we nourish the creator and mentor within us through a pensive solitude, which allows both for disciplined crafting of our gifts and communion with the multiple dimensions of existence.

Additionally, it is instructive to note the paradoxical situation that Chiron is taught, and then teaches, both the arts of warfare *and* healing. In fact, Chiron trains the greatest of Greek warriors—Achilles, Hercules, Jason—as well as the eventual Greek god of healing, Asclepius.

This means that Chiron, like all healers, knows *how to wound* and *how to heal*. In the area or aspect of life inflicted with pain and suffering, we can both wound others *and ourselves* due to the acute focus and attention to this area.

Why would we wound ourselves? It is similar to when we cut ourselves and begin to bleed. We stop. We stare. Our attention is arrested by the crisis at hand. This enhanced attention, which seeds *intentional* action, is the reason we may unconsciously wound ourselves.

The wound, and the necessary means of healing, often manifests through what we may call 'daimonic' situations, those events which remind us about our soul's karma, mission, and fate. The Shamanic Artist sustains a "chironic" awareness, perceiving the events and people surrounding our planetary *transits* as the soul's daimonic navigation system at play. Thus, our higher self—our Angel of Light—operates through the planetary transits—those effects of the sky's current position towards the unfolding of destiny inscribed in our birth chart.

Animal Medicine

Moments and motifs in our life erupt in those experiences of crisis which produce personal and collective epiphany or revelation. Often it is synchronistic experiences, even the challenging ones, which bring deep, personal meaning. These moments claw open our hearts to the divine architecture underlying and unifying all reality.

In one of the myths regarding Chiron's own physical wounding, a centaur crawls into Chiron's cave, struck by a poisonous arrow after a skirmish with Hercules. When Chiron goes to help him, he is cut by the poisonous arrow and suffers extreme agony. This is an interesting metaphor for the wounded animal part of ourselves, often repressed and locked inside due to our civilized culture, city life, and alienation from nature and her cycles.

Acknowledging and honoring our animal natures is a central invitation of the Wounded Healer. The shamanic lens of Chiron can help us receive clarity, guidance, and information through attuning to our power animals—those archetypal forces which also carry the wisdom and soul-map of our personal daimon.

As we witness the repeating presence of animal spirits in our lives, it increases our sixth sense, attuning us to the transpersonal, spiritual forces at play. We ask, why does this animal appear now? What archetypal energy does this animal represent? How does it reflect my thoughts, emotions, relationships, and desires at this time in my life?

If you have not yet accessed the presence of your luminous higher self through power animals, you can think to any animals which have visited you in dreams or visionary experiences. Or you may consider animals you used to love as a child. The purity of this connection suggests a strong spiritual bond.

I used to love the Wolf as a young boy, yet I never had a dog. It wasn't until I turned 30 that the Wolf returned back into my life as a profound and deeply emotional symbol of home for me. Upon my move to Colorado, the state I now call home, Wolf appeared through the names of girlfriends, friends, street signs, in visionary journeys, and numerous other symbols. As a pack animal, Wolf's appearance always suggests to me that I am home and with my tribe.

Shamanic Consciousness perceives an animistic multiverse, repeatedly showering us with transdimensional messages, notes from the beyond, the betwixt, and the between. The animal realm is consistently a poignant affirmation of transpersonal awareness and layers of spiritual significance.

Owl is one of my foremost totems, tattooed over my heart. I was incredibly excited during a trip to Portland, OR, when I watched the fantastic movie The *Legend of the Guardians*, about a group of Owls out to heal and save the world through the power of magic and following their dreams.

On the day I left Portland, my friend showed me a full-size stuffed owl, something I had never before seen. Upon arrival back home in Denver that day, checking my email, a dear beloved of mine wrote about her dream the night before where three Owls were intently staring at her, the center one reminding her of my energy. After reading the email, I unpacked my bags to find an Owl ring I had lost months ago in my suitcase on top of the book *Alchemy for Personal Transformation*. Yes. Owlchemy!!

Within a few days of this magical event, I went out to the dumpster behind my house for a normal deposit of trash. But instead, a black spray-painted Owl stared back at me from the side of the dumpster! I paused, in shock. It was as if I had been pinched by the talons of the Owl—not pierced, but arrested into serious attention and mystical connection, a player on the stage of what Timothy Leary, John Lilly, and Robert Anton Wilson called the CCC, the Coincidence Control Center.

As we listen ever deeper to these magical messages, we apply what Carlos Castaneda's Don Juan called "second attention." With this deeper attunement to the voices of synchronicity, this wide-angle lens of perception, our sacred path opens before us as a golden doorway promising our transcendent potential, and the frequency of communications from the Coincidence Control Center increases exponentially.

Pattern Recognition

When one applies the language of astrology upon one's wounds, then the *diachronistic* lens opens in addition to the synchronistic. To perceive diachronistically means to receive meaning *through* time. This is the nature of astrological wisdom, a science which delivers the medicine of pattern recognition. By studying what occurred the last time planets were in the position they are now or will be in the future, we can foresee not specific events, but the patterns of energy unfolding. This same analysis can be accomplished by studying the repeating patterns of the wound.

In my adult life, one of my challenging wounds has surrounded turmoil and change in the home. The process of writing this book was delayed quite a bit during a summer when I did not have a home for five months. I moved into a new home in October of 2011, when Mars, the planet of action, desire, and conflict, moved into my area of the home, the roots, and the foundation—the fourth house.

When I thought back to two years before, Mars was in the exact same position of the fourth house when I moved into my previous location. The aggressive and restless energy of Mars in the area of the home seemed to consistently demand a physical relocation for me. Now, with this knowledge, I can prepare for two years from now, when Mars once again enters my fourth house. I should either plan to move or travel at that time to fulfill Mars' raging need to wreak havoc and chaos in my astrological area of the home.

The repeating of the wound compels the journey into discovering the origins. Why does this wound keep repeating? Why does it show up, in this form, in *my* life? This feeling of separation intrinsic to the wounding, that this dagger repeatedly stabs me in this way, produces profound suffering. The suffering we endure because of a feeling of separation compels us to "make whole," the true meaning of healing.

But until we access the root and not simply the symptom of our dis-ease, we will continue to wound ourselves in order to craft our soul back to its Source. In turn, we cultivate a shamanic hero, a myth-maker navigating the cartography of the multidimensional soul.

Our interrogation carries us into familiar, but mysterious terrain: resonances, reverberations, patterns, bubblings from the unconscious. Often we cannot locate a wounding trauma in some moment of personal biography. For instance, certain phobias we may have had since a young child or a dream that repeats, a dream that feels nostalgic—these may be difficult to source in this lifetime.

Naturally we begin to ask about karma, other lifetimes, perhaps

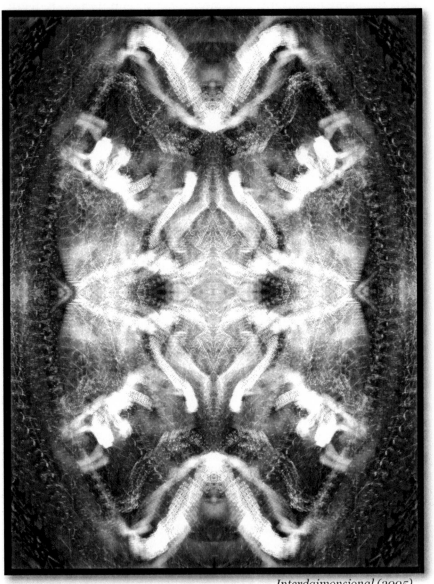

Interdaimonsional (2005)

the impact of our birth experience. Rebirthing, conscious breath-work, past-life regression, hypnotherapy, Emotional Freedom Technique—these are the languages the Wounded Healer within us can use to transcend the constrained roles of Saturnian reality and instead access our transpersonal nature, available through integrating the liberating freedom of Uranus, the visionary imagination of Neptune, and the transformational power of Pluto.

Chiron: From Earth Medicine to Astral Shaman

To master the earthly domain (Saturn), requires a knowledge of herbology, which Chiron cultivates, balancing his studies and subsequent wisdom of the celestial (Uranian) plane. By synthesizing the gifts of his grandfather and father, Chiron becomes a master of time and space and a teacher of astronomy and astrology. With these two sciences, Chiron crafts an art in which Time (Saturn-Chronos) becomes a revolutionary path for unleashing the soul's original and unique voice (Uranus).

But herbology is also used in a Uranian way, as astrology is used in a Saturnian way. For the knowledge of herbs, as witnessed in all indigenous cultures gives us the figure of the plant medicine shaman. Chiron thus embodies the Astral Shaman, an archetype seeking acknowledgment and integration today for modern psychedelic and consciousness explorers.

The birth chart functions not only as a map of the soul, but the planetary *transits* reflect the most appropriate and corresponding times for ceremony and ritual. Our ceremonial intentions are reflected in the archetypal energies represented by the planets. Thus a correspondence occurs between healing required, medicine applied, and archetypal (planetary) transit. The merger of sky and earth, through astrologically aligned ceremony is the Mayan, the Incan, the Egyptian, and the indigenous way of the Astral Shaman. The horoscope is not only a map for timing sacred ceremonies, but for integrating the expanded awareness which is born out of these experiences. Epiphanies and awakenings unfold while utilizing this integral language.

Chiron is a centaur, affiliated with a tribe of creatures who symbolize wild, instinctual powers. The Centaurs were always described as crazy and raucous beings, unconcerned with cultured, rational ways of behaving. We can reflect here upon the shadow expressions of the unconscious Uranus—a full throttle surge for freedom with often chaotic and traumatizing results.

But Chiron separates himself from this behavior. He develops the positive attributes of Uranus—individuality, innovative perspectives, a love of astrology and astronomy, and the cultivation of unique gifts and an original voice. Yet he is also civilized and wise, and fulfills a duty to serve humanity. These qualities represent the best aspects of the responsible Saturn figure, offering integrity and accountability in a role assisting the entire planet.

Also, the planet Uranus represents the innovations in technology. Weaponry is a kind of technology, and Chiron taught weaponry. Technology can be used to assist, evolve, and unite us, or it can be used to control, destroy, and numb us. Similarly the Wounded Healer has the ability to both wound and to heal. Today, Chiron teaches how our continuously shifting technological paradigms can be used to either harm or liberate us.

Chiron's use of weaponry in the hunt is also a metaphor for how to *use our resources efficiently and sustainably*. Chiron is the healer in each of us recognizing our interdependence on all of Mother Earth's resources. His hybrid nature is reflected in the unfolding paradigm of hybrid and electric vehicles—the synthesizing of energetic resources that help us to access more personal freedom and creative resilience, in a way that benefits the collective—a major theme of the emerging Aquarian Age.

CHAPTER 6

The Sacred Face of Sacrifice:
The Shaman's Call, the Artist's Torch

THE DRAGON'S LOVER

This past life
imprisonment
I don't need
to wound my self again
With this past life
dismemberment
Time to release
this karmic attachment...

Chiron!
Take the arrow from your thigh
And, admit and allow that you must die
on,
Into immortal realms
of sky
as constellation's sacred guide.

(Follow this LINK http://soundcloud.com/verdarluz to listen)

Journal Entry 3/11/11

I cannot do this.

The word FAIL is smeared boldface capslock all across my inner eye. Blood-red, dripping. Give-up. Too young. Not ready. Almost, but not quite.

There is a tree inside me trying to be born, but I am not on earth. I am drowning in this dimension, but trying to kill gravity and anchor in starlight. I must traverse space and time, for that star sung its saving rope to me how many light years ago?

The creative process IS the creation.

And I am being processed. I am being blended. I am shred apart and torn as I am being born...

Besides his wounded condition as an orphan and his exiled predicament from the other centaurs and from humans, Chiron was also *physically* wounded. In the most famous of the stories, the hero Hercules was invited to dinner by the Centaurs. Drink was passed around, as it often was with the rowdy Centaurs, and a fight erupted between Hercules and the Centaurs. Hercules fired a poisonous arrow at one of the Centaurs, and accidentally struck *his teacher* Chiron in the thigh. As an immortal, he could not die, so he suffered continuously for the rest of his long life.

The only way Chiron could free himself from the chronic wound is to sacrifice his immortality, which he does in exchange for the life of Prometheus—the Titan chained to a rock for stealing fire from the gods and gifting it to humanity.

If Chiron allows his own death, humanity will be liberated, and his suffering will end. Because of his compassion, Chiron sacrifices himself. And because he elevated his suffering through the act of service, Chiron became one, and for some scholars, two of the constellations above—Sagittarius and Centaurus.

This aspect of Chiron's myth is very instructive for us. First, the "accidental" component reflects the common theme in both shamanism and the hero's journey of being *chosen* for a spiritual mission without personal volition. The word *avatar*, which has been used in television, film, and as a virtual internet identity, actually means "the chosen one." We are the chosen ones, the ones we have been waiting for, as the Hopis say. Thus, we cannot resist our avataric role, just as the shaman cannot ignore the vocation to heal. Like the hero of all narrative journeys, we may wish to refuse the call as we feel reluctance to fulfill our missions here. Fear may prevent us from fulfilling our creative duties. But *A Course in Miracles* teaches that:

> *All aspects of fear are untrue because they do not exist at the creative level and therefore do not exist at all. To whatever extent you are willing to submit your belief to this test, to that extent, are your perceptions corrected.*

If what we had previously perceived as an accident was now perceived as a creative necessity, a plot twist intended to awaken us into our higher life purpose, then we could release all blame and embrace our present moment, convinced of that golden Piscean motto that *all is perfect because it is happening*. With this conviction, we may accept our roles as creative healers. Robert Ryan describes this element of shamanic initiation in his book, *The Strong Eye of Shamanism*:

> *A shamanic vocation is obligatory. One cannot refuse it. The call of the forefathers and the illness are one and the same until the summons is acknowledged, for it was also the 'sickness that forced me to this path,' and it is similarly the voice of the sacred that is curative.... When I had no more strength to suffer, finally I agreed to become a shaman. And when I became a shaman I changed entirely.*

Sometimes a premonitory dream that overpowers the known perceptions, sometimes an illness that carries you to death's gaping door, and always the litmus test of your personal limits—the shamanic-artist's initiation pushes you to the edge of your capacity to be created by what you create.

Chiron is wounded by his own student. Likewise, we shamanic artists are wounded by our creations. Though our work may inspire others, we often must suffer through our creative process, as we learn how to allow what needs to be birthed through us to at last take shape, and morph our own souls in the process.

> *There will be many times when we won't look good—to ourselves or anyone else. We need to stop demanding that we do. It is impossible to get better and look good at the same time.*
>
> — *Julia Cameron, The Artist's Way*

Like the shaman, the artist receives the vision, the musician receives the song. We remember that Chiron taught music as well. But more importantly, he taught the need for devotion to our artistic craft, and humility and patience in the process of receiving the Creator *through us*. For, never are we so close to our Source as in the act of creation: the mother in labor pains, the musician channeling the

song, the teacher communicating the guiding message. We recognize that our entire creative process— each paint stroke, each guitar riff, each written verse, each crochet needle, each photo—is a gesture of return towards wholeness, towards Source, towards the spark that continuously creates the eternal flame.

Shamans often have spirit-lovers who can call the shaman to his vocation in dreams or visions. These spirit-lovers can even co-habit with the shamans and become quite possessive of them. Like a spirit-lover, the muse grabs hold of the artist and she will not release her fiery grip.

> *A person must pay dearly for the divine gift of creative fire. It is as though each of us was born with a limited store of energy. In the artist, the strongest force in his make-up, that is, his creativeness, will seize and all but monopolize this energy, leaving so little over that nothing of value can come of it. The creative impulse can drain him of his humanity to such a degree that the personal ego can exist only on a primitive or inferior level and is driven to develop all sorts of defects-ruthlessness, selfishness ("autoeroticism"), vanity, and other infantile traits. These inferiorities are the only means by which it can maintain its vitality and prevent itself from being wholly depleted.*

> —Carl Jung, "Psychology and Literature" (1930).

The voice that calls cannot be ignored, like the irresistible song of the Sirens as Homer's Odysseus sailed near their island. In his book *The Philosophers' Secret Fire*, scholar Patrick Harpur suggests that the muse "is a seductive source of inspiration and a dangerous, demanding sorceress....a daimon who once awakened, will try to become the centre of the personality."

The word "demon" actually originated from the term "daimon or deamon," and our modern conception of this term as evil is a degradation of the original term. As Professor E.R. Dodds describes, "Virtually everyone, pagan, Jewish, Christian or Gnostic, believed in the existence of these beings and in their function as mediators, whether he called them daemons or angels or aions or simply 'spirits.' As Christianity began to rise, the subtleties of the various daimons and spirits were ripped away, and the world became divid-

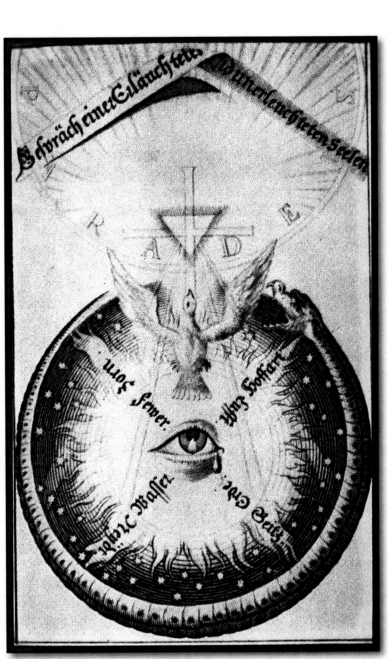

Jakob Boehme, from Theosphische Werke

ed into convenient descriptions of "evil" and "good." The positive function of the daimons was neglected and ignored as the Church deemed them all demonic agents of the devil.

Yet, before this dualistic split, the daimon was most often perceived as a force which continuously compels you to follow your destiny. Some say that our genius comes from the wisdom of our daimon, which knows the very core of our soul. But this genius cannot be fit into a neat and tidy category, for it exists as both a gift and a curse. It is both a tether to a daunting and overwhelming domain of imagination, and a ladder to the soul's ascension. Harpur notes that "Both W.B. Yeats and Carl Jung speak of her [the muse] in similar terms, as daimon who ruthlessly had their way with them, whom they had no choice but to follow, often to the detriment of their human life; and whom they struggled with and wooed all their days."

Thus, upon receiving our call, the shamanic artists and heroes of healing, must learn to forgive ourselves first. We are empowered by forces we cannot totally understand and we must sacrifice ourselves to these forces in order to serve, heal, and create. We are in constant adjustment and adaptation. We must change, with life, and compassionately accept, and boldly live our scripts. Our birth charts demonstrate the recipe for that unique healing brew, the cup that passeth before us in the cosmic drama.

> *If you're really listening, if you're awake to the poignant beauty of the world, your heart breaks regularly. In fact, your heart is made to break; its purpose is to burst open again and again so that it can hold evermore wonders.*
>
> — *Andrew Harvey*

Shedding Skin to Seed Creation

Delving deeper into Chiron's myth, we discover that the arrow from Hercules which struck Chiron was dipped in the poisonous blood of the Hydra, a many-headed *serpent-like* water beast. Hercules encountered the Hydra during one of his many famous labors. Every time he sliced off one of the Hydra's heads, nine more would grow.

The solar hero Hercules tries to destroy the Hydra by sheer strength and endangers himself more in attempting this. The only way Hercules could destroy the beast was to *lay down* before it and raise it into the air. This story's lesson teaches us that we must first learn to humble ourselves. Experiencing the repeating manifestation of our deepest wounds is our window into where to begin.

Humility demands that we release our resistances in order to surrender before the instinctual and unconscious realms. If we do not, then the repressed or ignored demons/daimons of the unconscious will multiply and wage havoc on us. This is why the embrace and awareness of one's unconscious **Shadow,** the Hydra within, is a core goal for the Wounded Healer. Jung describes the importance of owning our darker nature:

> *Everyone carries a shadow, and the less it is embodied in the individual's conscious life, the blacker and denser it is. If an inferiority is conscious, one always has a chance to correct it. Furthermore, it is constantly in contact with other interests, so that it is continually subjected to modifications. But if it is repressed and isolated from consciousness, it never gets corrected.*

Ironically, it is this "accidental" wounding which serves Chiron's spiritual purpose while on earth. Hercules, the student, plays the role of the "wounder," awakening Chiron, the teacher, to his higher vocation and service. As Chiron discovers that he cannot heal himself, he actually deepens his knowledge and ability about how to heal others. For, if Chiron had not been inflicted by the arrow with the Hydra's blood—that serpentine image, always connected to the writhing life force of the unconscious—then he would not have gone on the search to heal his wounds and gifted others the great service of his teaching. In releasing his grip on his immortal nature, Chiron realizes that his true freedom will come once he sacrifices his chronic wound. In his willingness to release his suffering and pain, and in his compassion for humanity, Chiron then achieves immortality amongst the stars.

In a sense, Chiron's willing death *births* the entirety of human creativity, since his sacrifice for Prometheus unleashes the magic of fire for all humanity. In addition, Chiron taught Asclepius the arts of healing, which passed down through Asclepius' daughters Hygeia and Panacea, eventually creating the entire guild and lineage of medical doctors. Thus, the potent reverberation of our sacrifice may never be known at its largest scale by us, but the domino effects ripple out to the evolution of all species, reminding us of the Buddhist Bodhisattva Vow: to postpone personal enlightenment in order to save all sentient beings.

This is an essential message for the heroic artists and healers of today. For our arts have become modalities to instruct and heal. And our healing work continues to inspire the next level of creativity. As we shed our limited self-definitions and rebirth ourselves through our creations and healing practices, we can ascend to even greater heights, becoming a constellation as Chiron did—shining, guiding, and inspiring others.

CHAPTER 7

Crafting The Middle Way

The Tripartite Storyteller: Actor, Playwright, Narrator

In one sense, we have all lied to ourselves in order to incarnate at all. For this phenomenal world is, according to the Vedantic Hindus "maya," an illusion. Similarly, in the Buddhist perception, all phenomena are "empty," that is, without a self-nature. Our spiritual test on the earth plane is to recognize and accept the illusion of separation as necessary in order to serve others. Amidst the seductive impermanence of relative reality, our service culminates in the reminder of this ultimate truth of luminous unity, from the tiniest quark to the unfathomable vastness of the Multiverse.

On our path of awakening, we discover then that it is the myth we scribe each day about ourselves which will either imprison us in the sickness of separation, or liberate us in the wild freedom of spiritual re-union.

What we arrive at here is a model of the soul's incarnate journey and tri-partite nature. First, in the body, we are the ACTOR. This is the decree of our Fates we mentioned earlier, the collection of karmas we must fulfill. We wrote this karma with our previous actions and are currently writing the script of our future incarnations. Thus, we are also the PLAYWRIGHT, as well as the actor.

The third part is the Chiron test, as to whether the Wounder, Wounded, or the Healed will tell the story. For we are the NARRATOR. It is our tone of voice, our inflection in our reactions, and our relationship to our role and our experiences in that role which determines our soul's evolution.

This is the alchemical artist, like the bards of ancient days, attending to the voiceover that stirs in every moment. In the Buddhist Eightfold Path, this attention of the Shamanic Artist is called Right View. Right View can also be called "right outlook" and involves the cultivation of correct perception—the affirmation that all is interdependent, so nothing exists separately, nor permanently. Right View extends to mean that we may also perceive all those people, experiences, and life situations we encounter as teachers, messengers, guides, and foremost: beneficial reflectors of healing potential. Words, ideas, relationships, touch, laughter, the cool breeze, the bark of the tree, and even the argument, the traffic jam, the loss of a home—all of these serve our higher purpose, and are somehow part of the destiny which our daimon helps us to fulfill.

For it isn't what happens *to* us that is of the highest importance. Instead, the *stories we share about our fate* determine our spiritual development. In our role as narrator, we must develop Right View, which challenges us to ask whether our story will be a separating or a unifying force.

If our story separates us from our Source, then we fall into the quicksand traps of Wrong View. We become the disempowered victim and we will attach to the wounded story. We will pull the trigger at the image in the mirror. We will hang ourselves upon the hook that nails us to the cross of suffering.

If instead, we can cultivate Right View as the narrator of our own life, then in our role as playwright, other precepts to end our suffering, such as Right Thought and Right Speech will naturally unfold. With Right Thought (also called Right Intention), we resolve to being here, *on purpose*. We recognize that "What I am experiencing is a result of what I am thinking and feeling." And out of these positive thoughts will arrive the speech that supports us and those around us. There is no room for gossip or complaint. This returns us to the alchemical role of positive affirmations in living a fulfilling life. A Course in Miracles reminds us, "What you are experiencing is a result of what you are thinking/feeling...The only place that you can exercise choice is thought... What you do comes from what you think" And by extension, what you say derives from what you think.

The other aspects of the Noble Eightfold Path—Right Livelihood, Right Effort, Right Mindfulness, and Right Concentration—all begin and end upon the pillar of Right View, whose foundation is the Four Noble Truths. The Wounded Healer perseveres in Right View. This archetype within us lives the principles of the Eightfold Path through persistent realization of the Four Noble Truths:

1. Life is suffering.
2. The origin of suffering is attachment.
3. The cessation of suffering is attainable.
4. There exists a path to the cessation of suffering, the Middle Way, described in the Eightfold Path

The Wounded Healer recognizes how his own suffering occurs repeatedly and how it hooks him. He hunts for the hurt and traumatized parts, with the warrior's awareness that *the way out is through* the very area of painful attachment. Without indulgently identifying with our stories of defeat, nor completely trying to ignore or distract ourselves from our sacred medicine, the Shamanic Artist rides the shifting tide of the Middle Way.

The Art of Abiding and Aspiring

Much Buddhist teaching reflects the essence of the Wounded Healer and Shamanic Artist's goal. It is summarized in two concepts: abiding and aspiring, which pulse as the heart of the Tonglen practice.

The goal of the Buddhist Tonglen practice, as described by Buddhist nun, Pema Chodron, is to directly contact the suffering and joy of human existence and to realize the universality of these states of being. In Tonglen, we avoid doing the habitual behaviors which always paralyze us: the compulsion to push away that which is painful and cling to that which is pleasurable. Tonglen reverses this pattern.

Instead, when it's painful we breathe it in, own it, and allow ourselves to be touched by it without being torn apart by it. When it's pleasurable, we loosen our grip on the moment we so cherish, and send a wish that others may share in the sense of joy or delight that we are feeling.

In order to practice Tonglen, we must first root ourselves in *maitri*, the practice of compassion or unconditional friendship towards oneself. Yet, more often, a situation of tension arises, the wound surfaces, and we react with unconscious aggression. In Buddhism, it is called "shenpa," which refers to the qualities, the stories, and the triggers that hook us. Shenpa is how we get stuck, and reveals all of our attempts to escape the situation through addictive behaviors with food, shopping, alcohol, drugs, sex, and work.

But if we practice maitri, we befriend ourselves and learn to abide in the situation, feeling, or wound as it is. We remain, persist, and sustain ourselves through the difficulty. For every time we feed the defeat and react, we strengthen our attachment to the trigger or wound. The more consciousness and insight one has by remaining with the wound-as-friend, the more that integration and awakening is a real possibility and the less energy you have to waste in reaction to the circumstance. In this practice, we realize that the painful reactions are not productive, nor creative.

Usually, when the shenpa arises, we denigrate and criticize ourselves for having the negative emotion. But the Wounded Healer alchemy requires instead that we rejoice in this abiding. We celebrate the aspect within ourselves which witnesses the wound. We then aspire to discipline ourselves in the language of abiding, for it is this quality of inner stillness which allows the compassionate heart to blossom. This open and liberated heart is the secret key to fulfilling the Tonglen practice to breathe in the suffering and wish that others be relieved of that same pain, or to breathe out the joy we feel and send it to all sentient beings.

CHAPTER 8

The Shamanic Alchemist

The greatest weight.—What, if some day or night a demon were to steal after you into your loneliest loneliness and say to you: 'This life as you now live it and have lived it, you will have to live once more and innumerable times more; and there will be nothing new in it, but every pain and every joy and every thought and sigh and everything unutterably small or great in your life will have to return to you, all in the same succession and sequence - even this spider and this moonlight between the trees, and even this moment and I myself. The eternal hourglass of existence is turned upside down again and again, and you with it, speck of dust!' Would you not throw yourself down and gnash your teeth and curse the demon who spoke thus?...Or how well disposed would you have to become to yourself and to life to crave nothing more fervently than this ultimate eternal confirmation and seal?

—*Friedrich Nietzsche*

Roller Coaster Medicine

The healing journey is like a roller coaster ride you will not exit from. At first, your stomach turns in queasy uncertainty as you drop from the great heights and get spun and whiplashed. You cry and then you laugh; you break down before you break through. And then, as the ride continues and you notice your reactions, you begin to reach an inner calm, a stillness, a locus of equanimity where no valley's jaws can consume you, no overwhelming peak can move your tranquil Witness. You are still on the ride, but you are not slammed against the metal bars. If you choose to scream and release and toss your arms about in catharsis, then you CHOOSE this, because it's the most appropriate mode of healing.

Integrating Chiron's Wounded Healer lessons, you can ask yourself: What is the evolutionary intention of this? How would I wish to re-experience this crisis moment during my life review, in my final breaths, in my moment of transition at death? How would I *act* here, instead of *react*? What words would I vibrate out, what thoughts would I emanate?

With Chiron, we learn that we must *choose to be the chosen ones.* To become the shamanic hero, we must conquer ourselves and venture beyond the limits of what we thought possible. In alchemy, this pivotal moment is related to *Separatio,* the third stage of the Great Opus—the act of turning the lead weight of the wounded soul into the feathered serpent healer of fiery gold.

We discover, however, that we have usually been inundated by the first two stages of the alchemical opus, the *Calcinatio* and *Dissolutio.* The challenge of these two stages is encompassed in a quote from A Course in Miracles "All fear is fear of change." Yet we know that change is truth and fear is the pattern of holding on. Truth is letting go into impermanence.

In **Calcinatio,** the individual's belief systems and defense mechanisms are sacrificed in the purifying fire. The ego's former authority begins to burn away as the soul realizes the material illusions it has embraced..

On the chemical level, calcination is the reduction of the substance by fire, heating it until it is reduced to ash. If we were to take an herb, the calcination would be the grinding and roasting of the herb. The evolutionary lesson involved in Calcination is the realization that through the power of fire, we can destroy all things that are not essential.

On a psychological level, the destruction of the fixed patterns in the rational mind threatens all the ego holds dear, and the initiate at this stage often experiences depression, hopelessness, and defeat.

In calcinatio, we begin to shatter the crystallized elements of the personality and the attachments of the self to its limited belief systems. Every resistance surfaces as the ego battles ferociously to defend its role, its mask, its status quo of habitual patterning, to no avail against the onrushing flames of the transforming fires.

Then in **Dissolutio,** the initiate drowns in the all-consuming

forces of the unconscious. In this stage, solid substances are absorbed in liquids. The alchemist would take the ashes from the calcination and dissolve them in water or liquid chemicals. This act of watery purification, such as the baptism and cleansing rituals of many religions and spiritual practices, returns a substance or an individual back to their original, undifferentiated state, the primordial pools of the psyche.

What we thought was a solid self becomes flooded with archetypal powers, gods, goddesses, forces beyond one's control. Even the juices of lust and love, like sirens or mermaids, threaten to liquify the fixed and static aspects of the personality. Stages of psychological development can often not be accomplished until one is confronted by love's vast and daunting ocean.

The flood myths from cultures around the world universally speak of a Divine Source sending the floods when humanity has become tainted and degenerate. The wicked are to be destroyed, and the righteous who have lived an authentic existence are to be saved. On a psychospiritual level, the negative detritus of the inflated ego must be dissolved away. Only those elements of the personal self willing to be encompassed and aligned with the Absolute Self will survive.

Separatio and Eternal Recurrence

The phase of Separatio (separation) can initially begin with a brutal recognition. It is a resounding thunderchord of conviction that we are separated from our Source.

Birth itself imprints this separation anxiety, for not only do we leave the warm enclosed nursery of the womb, but in the cutting of the placental cord, we are literally separated and removed from our *source* of nourishment. As infants, we immediately experience a sense that we are not enough, that we are insufficient, and that we are very vulnerable.

Over the years, this sense of separation can manifest on both conscious and subconscious levels. Conditioned by our cultures, our schools, and often our families, we are told that we are different and separate from other nationalities, or religions, genders, the earth, our creator, or love itself. In order to survive, we all employ what astrologer and Chiron expert, Adam Gainsburg calls, "devices of protection" to attempt to shield ourselves from this impending sense of separation.

If we have remained in a subconscious belief of our separate state, we may at this alchemical phase attract in a teacher, a lover, a stranger, or a life circumstance which acts as the *healer who wounds*. This person or experience acts as an evolutionary force we attract in which serves to sever us from the ignorance or naïveté which consciously believes that all is ok, yet below the surface recognizes a split both within oneself and between oneself and the world.

This repeated "wounding" and the recognition of the pattern is necessary to begin the individual on their path towards healing, and eventual wholeness. Yet, over time, our shell of innocence has been ruptured, and the open heart has broken. It is crucial in this stage that the initiate remember that the only heart worth having is a broken one. In other words, as Gainsburg reminds us, "the wisdom only shows up when we remain courageous in the breaking open, instead of shutting down."

Thus, in separatio, the shamanic alchemist must cultivate the disciplined and determined *will towards self-transcendence*, invited by Nietzsche's invitation to overcome oneself

When one has developed a healthy sense of personal space and boundary, through a focused intent, then can the shamanic hero truly guide the will of the third chakra upward, through the broken, but open heart into the next stage of *coniunctio* (conjunction).

One needs to distance oneself from the world, and in so doing, also objectify from one's own processes. The creative function necessarily is a severing. In most cosmogonic myths, Father Sky and Mother Earth must separate for creation to actually occur.

Likewise, in order for the storyteller to channel the inspiring narrative, he or she must separate from the collective in order to detach and determine the most important tale to tell, whatever genre, using whatever appropriate instrument from the artistic tool belt.

On the healing journey, we also must detach enough from our stories to gain the proper perspective of our wounds: as sacred gifts utilized to serve others.

Separatio can bring clarity, but can bring conflict, for we start to hear all the warring voices within and outside of us. When Jesus said, "I come not to bring peace, but a sword," the suggestion is that we have to slice away all that which is not essential, within ourselves and our relationships in order to reach an enlightened state of consciousness.

Separatio is an absolutely integral step in order for healthy relationships to be initiated and to endure, for often it is our uncon-

scious identification and habitual codependence on family, friend, employer, or lover that prevents us from truly living in the compassionate and loving heart.

The Uranian discord that can ensue from Separatio disturbs the Saturnian status quo in its stale serenity, its role-bound ignorance. We must sift through the illusions of our ego, divorce ourselves from it, and then apply the fires of the Holy Spirit to only that deemed worthy for redemption. We can ask for the assistance of Archangel Michael or the bodhisattva Manjushri. Both of these higher beings wield the sword of truth which cuts through the illusions of ego desires, false attachments, and dualistic thinking to arrive at transcendent wisdom. To invoke the presence of this energy, you can chant the mantra for Manjushri, believed to enhance wisdom and also improve one's skills in debating, memory, writing, and other literary abilities:

Om a ra pa sa na dhī

In this alchemical phase of separatio, we can think again of Chiron, in his cave, distant from others, but cultivating his special gifts and skills. This is also our "martial training," such as the training of the various pupils of Chiron. It is "martial" in the sense that Mars symbolizes our conscious desires. I *choose* to study or learn this various skill—art, music, healing, writing etc.—so that I can assist or serve others through it. This offering will in some way define my individuality, but as an integral part of the Whole. This is how the shamanic hero reconciles the potential alienation or anxiety of the emerging Aquarian Age: with the determined effort to apply his training to the role of embodied bodhisattva.

We know that we are the "avatars," the chosen ones, the ones we have been waiting for. But often, knowing our power as creators and healers, we are overwhelmed with our multidimensional awareness, our abundance of gifts to share, our desire to expand our auras into their infinite potential. This can challenge us to make decisions about where to apply our creative energy and how to develop our healing gifts. We wish to be of the highest service, but HOW?

The HOW is of the linear Mind, concerned with the Saturnian laws of space and time. The ego can't help but get involved here, as Saturn's role is to structure our consciousness outwardly, so that we may fulfill a role in the world. But instead of succumbing to Saturn's control issues and time obsessions, we would be best to use Saturn in order to strategize moments to maximize their potential benefit. For instance, we can use tools such as Electional Astrology to choose the most appropriate dates and times to start businesses, launch websites, and ceremonially commit to our beloved. After all, Saturn was Chronos in the Greek world—Father Time. The merger of Saturn and Uranus in the rulership of Aquarius, the sign associated most with astrology, demonstrates how a harmonic relationship to Time (Saturn) can function to awaken the Uranian magic—liberating us into realizing our unique gifts, accessing our original voice, and freeing ourselves from limited, consensus, or unconscious expressions of the archetypes.

Uranian intuition does seem to flow most when we do that which sustains the vibration of bliss. *Ananda*, or bliss, is a state experienced NOW, when Consciousness is aligned with the Truth of the present moment, not a projected future perfect state. The future always arrives with its own set of challenges. Fellow astrologer, Rob Brezny, reminds us to "Dream of all the masterpieces you'd be thrilled to create, but work on just one at a time."

This quote reminds us that we must be patient with our pathways of transformation. Thus, the Wounded Healer, the Shaman-Artist, by magnifying our apparent deficiency, we discover the very modality, art form, or skill that will be our greatest service towards others. This is by nature an alchemical process, whereby we shapeshift our pain and separation into its glorious gift to the world. We move from Separation to Conjunction.

Coniunctio and Returning to Wholeness

Jungian psychotherapist Edward Edinger writes, "Space for consciousness to exist appears *between* the opposites, which means that one becomes conscious as one is able to contain and endure the opposites within."

Separatio allows us the ability to call out our complexes and provide a linguistic mapping for our evolution. When we study our birth charts, we enact separatio, first by studying the elemental breakdown, noticing our constitutions. We may have a preponderance of the Air element, equated to the Thinking/Mental function and the Swords in the Tarot. Or we may be more immersed in the energies of Water and the Feeling state, symbolized by the Cups in the Tarot. Our recipe may include more or less of Sensation symbolized by the Pentacles in Tarot, representing the Earth element. Or our major ingredient may be Fire, source of the Intuitive Spirit and represented by the Wands.

As we divide and define more specifically, we notice that each planet in our astrology chart corresponds to a distinct intelligence inside of our psyche and an evolutionary urge in our soul. We are pluralities, composed of gods and goddesses: forces and intelligences that must negotiate between each other. As we attune ourselves to these inner voices, we recognize how we have projected those voices within out to others, attempting to blame. Again, at the end of the Piscean Age, this projecting part of us must wither away. We must allow the particular songs of each inner voice to channel through: their energetic expressions through their sign and house placement.

Also, each sign of the zodiac has its natural opposite, which acts as its teacher when one enters the shadow or dense expression of that sign. To dance the sign of polarity or the oppositions, squares, or conjunctions—the challenging aspects in one's chart—is a literal expression of the alchemical phase which occurs following the Sep aratio, the stage of the fourth chakra: *Coniunctio*.

In coniunctio, we must reconcile the opposing part of our psyche, the masculine King and feminine Queen, in order to birth our creative children. The ambitious drive of the Solar yang spirit must merge with the receptive art of the Lunar yin soul.

In this process, a sacred marriage occurs within the alchemist, whereby dualistic limitations—on one level, symbolized by gender—are transcended. This was often depicted in alchemical art as the Sun and Moon uniting in the sky or two white birds raising a crown into the heavens.

Integration of polarities is a primary purpose in all forms of Evolutionary and Shamanic Astrology. In the school of Evolutionary Astrology, the 180 degree polarity position of Pluto, by sign, house, and degree, correlates to the specific evolutionary intentions for this life of any individual. In addition, the opposite points of the Lunar Nodes—symbols of the soul's past life dynamics and current life intentions—express the lesson of coniunctio. Their opposition instructs us that one's advancement from karmic patterns to dharmic destiny and purpose is predicated on the ability to internalize and then outwardly express the opposition. Enacting therapeutic healing exercises, such as meditating upon or dancing the polarity positions of all one's planets could act as a great teaching on the path towards wholeness.

We may also consider the coniunctio as an invitation—amidst our despair and confusion, as well as our synchronicities and epiphanies—to reunite with our daimon, to stitch back together the lower self with its higher self, to allow that reactive ego to still itself and listen to its inner guidance.

Perhaps we can find a semblance of inner personal truth, here in the dance between opposites. In his book, *Strength to Love*, Martin Luther King Jr. explains the importance of integrating the lessons of coniunctio:

> *The strong man holds in a living blend strongly marked opposites...life at its best is a creative synthesis of opposites in fruitful harmony. The philosopher Hegel said that truth is found neither in the thesis nor the antithesis, but in the emergent synthesis which reconciles the two.*

Likewise, in a letter to Frau Olga Fröbe-Kapteyn, Carl Jung used alchemical metaphors to elucidate our intrinsic oppositional nature,

> *There can be only patient endurance of the opposites which ultimately spring from your own nature. You yourself are a conflict that rages in itself and against itself in order to melt its incompatible substances, the male and the female, in the fire of suffering and thus create that form which is the goal of life. Everyone goes through this mill, consciously or unconsciously, voluntarily or forcibly. We are crucified between the opposites and delivered up to the torture, until the reconciling third takes shape. Do not doubt the rightness of*

the two sides within you and let whatever may happen,
happen. The apparently unendurable conflict is proof
of the rightness of your life. A life without intercontra-
diction is either only half a life or else a life in the be-
yond which is destined only for angels.

When the opposites merge, the third that is reborn is the self of Wholeness.

The conjunction transcends the ego struggles of the "How" by uplifting the spirit into the open space of the unified "Intelligence of the Heart," as the Egyptians called it. Medieval alchemists referred to the blossoming of this perfect blend of thought and feeling as the intuitive wisdom of the "Philosopher's Child."

Thus, the will of the alchemist to *separate* his complexes and characters, allows him to listen to the individual voices so that they may *conjoin* together in one harmonious chorus. Astrology is the shamanic alchemist's language for this conjunction to the higher self, whereby we weave the multi-colored rainbow soul into one crystalline whole.

Shamanifest (2007)

CHAPTER 9

The Wounded Healer Lineage

We started this book with a reference to the thirteenth constellation, Ophiuchus, the Serpent-Bearer. This constellation represents Asclepius, the Greek God of Healing, whom Chiron taught. But the lineage of Divine Healers extends into many figures and traditions, including Archangel Raphael, the Medicine Buddha, and Christ, and into the healing path of the Hawaiian Huna tradition.

During a workshop with dream teacher, Robert Moss, he communicated that the first images of Christ resembled those of **Asclepius**.

For roughly 1500 years, those seeking healing made pilgrimage to the Asclepeion, located throughout the Mediterranean world. The cult of Asclepius became incredibly popular. At these healing sanctuaries, the patient would have to undergo Katharsis—ritual purification including a cleansing diet and bathing in sacred pools. The supplicant would spend their nights in prayer and dream incubation in the Abaton, or dream chamber, asking the god for a cure to their physical, mental, emotional, or spiritual illnesses. Asclepius, often in the form of a serpent, would commonly appear in the dream communicating a recommended cure. Or the dream would be shared with a priest of the temples who would prescribe the appropriate therapy after interpreting the dream.

It is important for us to consider this reference today, when many practitioners of shamanic healing work have made pilgrimage to the Amazon rainforest to work with shamans and the Amazonian plant medicine Ayahuasca. The serpent symbolism from the ancient Greek association with Asclepius translates to Ayahuasca as well, since the tree from which the sacred tea is made is shaped like a coiled DNA serpent.

One of the most powerful and common of visions which occur after the ingestion of Ayahuasca is the snake. In one of my journeys with Ayahuasca in Peru, I had asked the plant medicine teacher to show me a vision of the future, to help give me foresight into what was coming that I may teach it to help and guide others. I had gone up for a second cup of the medicinal tea with this question in my heart. As soon as I began to sip the second cup, the jaws of a massive serpent consumed and swallowed me whole.

The vision which followed this experience was less clear than the image of the snake, involving a sort of alien-looking species, a robotic intelligence, and humanity chasing after this elusive ball of energy. Perhaps this reflected a collective evolutionary movement towards some kind of free energy device.

As our shaman shared with us in the integration afterwards, when an animal comes to swallow you in the visionary space, it is that being's invitation to you to become your guide. That species has medicine, wisdom, and instruction for you that you cannot ignore.

The following is an introduction to the lineage of the Wounded Healer, communicated in the voice of Asclepius.

"PARENTS. AND THE REASONS WE CHOOSE THEM.

IT COULDN'T GET MORE INTENSE THAN MY FATHER, MOST HOLY, AND SO MOST FEARFUL: APOLLO. HE THREW MY MOTHER ONTO THE FIRE, NEARLY KILLING ME IN THE PROCESS. FORTUNATELY, HE HAD ENOUGH WITS ABOUT HIM TO SEND DOWN HERMES TO RIP ME OUT OF THE WOUND AND BRING ME TO SAFETY JUST IN TIME. THIS PRETTY MUCH MADE ME THE FIRST C-

SECTION IN HISTORY. MY NAME, ASCLEPIUS, MEANS "TO CUT OPEN."

SO HOW'S THAT FOR A BIRTH TRAUMA?! SLICED FROM THE WOMB, MY MOTHER KILLED BY MY RAGING FATHER– YOU KNOW THE STORY? LIKE MANY OF YOU WITH MOTHERS NOT ABLE TO NURTURE YOU, OR AN ABSENT FATHER WHO LEFT THE SCENE IN VIOLENCE AND NEVER EVEN SAW MY FACE.

THIS IS THE CHALLENGE AND BLESSING FOR ALL OF US DEMI-GODS AND LIGHT-WORKERS. IT'S THAT STING OF ORPHANAGE—PARENTS, SOCIETY, SCHOOL—ALL OF WHICH ABANDONED US.

BUT WE HAVE OUR SURROGATE FAMILIES, OUR KINDRED SOULS, SCOURING THE HEAVENS FOR MEANING, SCAVENGING THE EARTH FOR PURPOSE. TEACHERS AND MENTORS AND ANGEL-GUIDES APPEAR IN EACH PERSON YOU MEET. FOR ME IT WAS MY FOSTER FATHER, THE WISE CENTAUR CHIRON.

FROM CHIRON, I LEARNED THE DELICATE ART OF THE WOUNDED HEALER. CHIRON TAUGHT ME HOW TO TRANSMUTE MY PAIN, AND OFFER MY SUFFERING AS MY SPECIAL MEDICINE TO HELP OTHERS. THE MOST IMPORTANT LESSON THAT CHIRON TAUGHT ME WAS THAT WE ARE NEVER FULLY HEALED, BUT WE ARE ALWAYS HEALING, THAT IS, WE ARE EVER STRIVING TOWARDS WHOLENESS, RETURNING TO UNION.

CHIRON TOO WAS WOUNDED LIKE I, ORPHANED AND EXILED. PERHAPS THIS IS WHY MY FATHER APOLLO SENT ME TO HIM TO BE RAISED.

THE REASON WHY ALL MYTHICAL GODS ABANDON THEIR CHILDREN, THE DEMI-GODS, IS FOR US DEMI-GODS TO CHOOSE TO RE-UNITE WITH OUR ANCESTRY THROUGH THE SHAMAN'S HEROIC JOURNEY, WHICH INCLUDES FIRST, THE INNER TURMOIL, A RECOGNITION OF ORPHANAGE FROM YOUR SOURCE, A SENSE OF BEING EXILED FROM OTHERS, AND THEN THE EMBARKING ON THE QUEST FOR SELF-REDEMPTION, NOT THE PROJECTION OF A SAVIOR OUTSIDE OF YOU.

IF YOUR PARENTS DID NOT ABANDON YOU OR GIVE YOU THAT CONFUSING LOOK: LOVE WITHOUT UNDERSTANDING—HOW COULD YOU NOT FIND YOUR UNIQUE PATH AND VOICE? IN THIS SAME WAY, I COULD NOT BECOME THE GOD OF HEALING UNLESS I FIRST RECOGNIZED MY OWN WOUNDS.

BUT TO LEARN THESE LESSONS, TO RELEASE ANGER AND RESENTMENT? WE ARE FRAGILE IN THIS PROCESS. TO APPRECIATE ALL THAT HAS BEEN AND WILL BE AS NECESSARY ELEMENTS OF THE LIFE YOU SCRIPT FOR YOURSELF, THE TEACHINGS YOU GIVE TO YOURSELF, TAKES A PROFOUND LEVEL OF MATURITY AND A WILLINGNESS TO EMBARK ON THE HEALING JOURNEY.

WE NEED OUR GUIDES, MENTORS, COACHES, TEACHERS, AND HEALING DEITIES, TO REMIND US THAT WE HAVE CHOREOGRAPHED IT ALL, THAT THE UNIVERSE IS CONSPIRING TO HELP US BECOME MORE WHOLE. THIS IS WHAT HEALING MEANS: A VOYAGE TO WHOLENESS. AND SO SHAMANIC ARTIST, I INVITE YOU TO EMBRACE THE MESSAGE OF THE WOUNDED HEALER...."

Asclepius had five daughters, four of which performed a particular function of the healing arts. **Panacea** was the goddess of universal remedy, who retained a poultice which could cure all ills. Her sister, **Hygeia** personified health, cleanliness, and sanitation. **Iaso** assisted in the recuperation from illness. Another sister, **Aceso**, oversaw the entire process of healing, as one endured its tests of patience and persistent spirit.

To the Mayans, **Ix Chel** is Lady of the Rainbows. She is considered the Moon goddess and thus, associated with fertility. She was the foremost of female deities in the Mayan tradition, a goddess of midwifery and medicine, and like Asclepius, often represented with a serpent. While Chel means "rainbow" in the Yucatan language, her prefix, Ix, refers to the day sign in the Mayan calendar of the Jaguar, representative of the shaman-kings, associated with leadership and healing. Ix Chel then is the Queen Shamaness of the Mayan tradition and teacher of the healing wisdom and regenerative power of cycles.

In the Celtic tradition, **Brigid** is the goddess of poetry, smithcraft, and healing. She is honored annually in the celebration of the pagan cross quarter day, Imbolc, every February first to second. The word "imbolc" was taken from the phrase "in the belly," and refers to that which we are becoming pregnant with during the winter's long gestation. Imbolc marks the midpoint of winter, halfway between the shortest day of the Winter Solstice and the rebirth of the Sun at the Spring Equinox. It is important that we purify at this time, so that the inner fires of creativity we tend to, may be shared with the world. Purifying herbs and oils include citronella, tea tree, and smudge sticks of sage. In order to purify, fire has always been the element of reverence during this festival. The lighting of fires symbolized the increasing power of the Sun over the coming months.

For the Christian calendar, this holiday was renamed 'Candlemas,' when candles are lit to remember the purity of the Virgin Mary. The veneration of the Virgin was borrowed from the honoring of the goddess Brigid, also known as Brighid, Bríde, Brigit, Bríd, We get the word 'brightness' from the name Brigid. Lighting the "sacred flame" of the candle, tending the hearth, sweat lodges, healing circles, sexual abstinence, fire meditations, storytelling, and poetry are all ideal ways to honor the bright spark of spirit being cultivated within ourselves during the heart of winter.

The lineage of the Wounded Healer also stretches back all the way to the primordial realms of the angels, for it is **Archangel Raphael** who provides healing for ourselves and the planet. In Hebrew, his name means, "God cures." His emerald green energy bestows the healing of the heart chakra and the color of spring rebirth—the generous and rejuvenating love of nature herself. The truth that Raphael represents is that all changes are helpful—they are necessary gifts which can continually spark epiphany within us, and wake us to the next phase of our sacred incarnate journey. Raphael can be called upon for assistance in healing, counseling, and safe guidance in travel.

Christ is the quintessential Wounded Healer figure, with remarkable similarities to Chiron. Both beings are immortals and eternally wounded. Christ is pierced in his side, Chiron is wounded in the leg by a poisonous arrow. Both are hybrid beings: Christ knows himself to be a god, Chiron knows himself to be a demi-god.

In *Supernatural*, Graham Hancock confirms this connection:

> *After its foundation around 2,000 years ago it was, at first, an overtly shamanistic religion. This is hardly surprising since Christ was so obviously and so profoundly a shaman. It is not only his pedigree as a half-human, half-divine hybrid that makes him so, or his heaven-sent gifts as a healer. His ordeal of crucifixion and piercing, followed by death and subsequent resurrection as a spiritualized being equipped with the power to save souls, is essentially the story of the wounded man – the story that is told by all shamans everywhere of their own initiatory agonies, death, and resurrection.*

Christ on the Cross also signifies the animal part of us, bleeding under the third-dimensional laws of space and time, symbolized by the cross of matter.

Upon the crucifix, Christ also echoes the theme of the orphaned child, emphasized in Chiron's myth. Christ pleads, "Eli, Eli, lama sabachthani!" or "My god, My God, why hast thou forsaken me?" But if we probe deeper, we discover a hidden layer of this phrase, as unveiled by The Nazarene Way of Essenic Studies.

> *The late Aramaic Bible researcher George Lamsa claimed that the traditional "forsaken" interpretation is a mistake in the Aramaic scribing that was transferred to later transcriptions. Lamsa claimed that "the correct translation from Aramaic should be "Eli, Eli, lemana shabakthani" or "My God, my God, for this [pur-*

pose] I was spared!" or "...for such a purpose have you kept me!") According to Lamsa's translation, rather than a "loss of faith" Christ meant to say "so this is my destiny."

And so we return to the Fates, the arbiters of our karma and revealers of our purpose. In the gospels of Matthew and Luke, the Fates communicate in the testing ground of the Garden of Gethsemane, Jesus tells his apostles "My soul is very sorrowful, even to death; remain here, and watch with me.' And going a little farther, he fell on his face and prayed, saying, 'My Father, if it be possible, let this cup pass from me; nevertheless, not as I will, but as you will" (Matthew 38, 39). In Luke, "And there appeared to him an angel from heaven, strengthening him. And being in an agony he prayed more earnestly; and his sweat became like great drops of blood falling down to the ground" (Luke 43, 44).

With the angel of strength, we can think here of the daimon, the guide reminding each one of us of our destiny, and that our suffering serves a higher purpose. Jesus's suffering reflects the Chiron condition within us, so aware of that repeating wound, the cross we have to bear, in order to assist others and gain the gold of compassion.

Twice, Jesus asked his disciples to keep watch with him and pray so that they would not fall into temptation, for "the spirit indeed is willing, but the flesh is weak." And still they slept.

Here, the sleeping disciples reflect those distracted and intoxicated aspects of our present-day humanity at the end of the Piscean age, as we project our messiah savior outside of us. As if seduced and then swallowed by the ocean's chaotic undertow, we often seek ecstasy, fantasy, or blind ignorance, unwilling to do the dedicated spiritual practices, the deep analysis, critique, and improvement of self and world, required of the spiritual devotee and sacred servant—that opposite sign of Pisces, Virgo.

At the end of the Piscean Age, in order to be a "disciple" of Christ-consciousness, we are required to "stay awake" at each moment, remaining *disciplined* in our spiritual practices and correct perception of our destiny, lest we fall into the Piscean temptations of blame, projection, and disassociation.

Above all, Christ's teachings and personal sufferings elucidate the revelation of the Wounded Healer and the craft of the Shamanic Artist—the need for compassion and loving service to all.

One of the historical meanings of the word Dharma, often used to refer to Buddhist teachings, is "that which heals." The historical buddha was often called the Supreme Physician, his teaching the Supreme Medicine, and the Sangha, or spiritual community, the Supreme Nurturers. The Buddha used health and disease as major metaphors for stages of spiritual awareness.

But physical healing alone could not cure the diseases in our minds or spirits. As past life regression therapy teaches, those afflictions of mind and spirit have the power to perpetuate themselves from one incarnation to the next. But if we use what Tulku Thondup Rinpoche calls "the four healing powers of the mind," we may be able to cure these ailments. These four healing powers include positive images, positive words, positive feelings, and positive beliefs.

These healing powers of the mind are applied in modalities of conscious breathwork, such as Transformational and Rebirthing, which use affirmations. With breathwork, the cells are overoxygenated, allowing for their regeneration. Stuck energy and old stories of defeat fixed in our etheric body and embedded in our cells begins to be released, and new healthy thought patterns can now be entrained into our consciousness. Since the breath is the first thing that we do in this life, and all of our births have some kind of fundamental trauma attached to them, breathwork helps to relieve that unconscious trauma and implement those positive, healing powers. We may need to hear and repeat to ourselves, that we are safe in this body or that we are beings of light traveling in the vehicle of the body.

In India, I saw a Tibetan doctor for some of my stomach ailments. I learned that Tibetan doctors pray to the **Medicine Buddha** at the beginning of each day. During my travels, I began a practice with the Medicine Buddha, including a Medicine Buddha empowerment, which I continue to this day. To embrace the four healing powers of the mind, you can invoke the Medicine Buddha using the practice of Deity Yoga: achieved through mantra, visualization, and sincere prayer.

A Tibetan Lama instructed me that the Medicine Buddha mantra could be done over dying animals, along with a sincere intention that those beings be reborn in their next life with the possibilities of a precious human rebirth. I have often applied this in those delicate moments on the road with animals who have been hit, or perhaps an insect drowning in the waters of the bathtub.

The mantra and visualization can be applied as well for all healers in their practice, before massage, teaching yoga, or doing any kind of counseling or energetic clearing. It is also a powerful invocation for our ceremonial work with plant medicines or as we hear of natural or manmade disasters affecting the earth and her species.

To begin the practice, find a comfortable seated position. Begin to chant the Mantra:

Teyata Om Bekanze Bekanze Mahabekanze
Radza Samud-Gate Soha

You can visualize the brilliant sky blue body of the Medicine Buddha, emerging out of the ethers, seated in a lotus position on a rainbow-colored lotus throne. He holds a myrobalan herb, a panaceaic plant. He offers this healing medicine to ease the sufferings of body and mind. His left hand rests in meditation mudra or posture, holding a monk's begging bowl filled with the healing elixir known as the "nectar of deathlessness."

Snow lions support his throne and symbolize the power and strength of the Buddha's commitment to heal all beings of the universe.

Teyata Om Bekanze Bekanze Mahabekanze
Radza Samud-Gate Soha

When reciting the Medicine Buddha mantra, pray for purification of all the wounded stories within you. Pray for the transformation of the triggers that cause your negative reactions

Bathe in that healing elixir and allow the toxic thoughts, the obscuring emotions, the karmic imprints, to all be cleansed. Allow the illusions to wash away and the darkness to evaporate.

With focus upon the Medicine Buddha, total balance, internal and external harmony, and spiritual peace can be attained, awakening the Supreme Physician, the enlightened Buddha within. The Medicine Buddha mantra reminds each of us of our Bodhisattva Vow: to serve all sentient beings.

Sentient beings are numberless,
I vow to free them.
Delusions are inexhaustible,
I vow to end them.
The Dharma Gates are boundless,
I vow to open them.
The Enlightened Way is unsurpassable,
I vow to embody it.

Huna, the Hawaiian indigenous shamanic tradition, is founded upon the concept of **Ho'oponopono**, which the Hawaiian Dictionary defines as "mental cleansing: family conferences in which relationships were set right through prayer, discussion, confession, repentance, and mutual restitution and forgiveness."

Essentially Ho'oponopono means "to make right." It can be applied to our ancestors and families, to our intimates and beloveds, and to ourselves. Ho'oponopono acts like alchemical transmutation as the Will is united with the Heart. The purpose is to correct the apparent wrongs that have occurred in one's life, including Hala (to miss the thing aimed for), Hewa (to go overboard or to extremes), and 'Ino (to do harm, whether intended or accidental).

To transcend the Piscean Age's residues of guilt and projection, it becomes essential at this turning of the Ages for the Wounded Healer in each one of us to exercise this all-encompassing forgiveness practice taught by the Huna shamans.

You can do this by creating a quiet and sacred space. Just allow any member of your family you struggle with, or any familial battle that has occurred to rise to the surface. Allow any ancestral illness or negative storyline to also rise. Say: I forgive you. I am sorry and I love you. Call forth your beloveds, all those who have shared the heart's embrace, whether for a single night, or for decades. Send them gratitude for your sharing and forgiveness for any of the wrongs incurred. And then look in the mirror. Stare with compassion. Go deep within yourself, within that tender pocket of grief, the anger, the resentment, the sorrow, the wound. Forgive it all. Say: "I love you and I release you."

As we cleanse the stuck triggers and repeating wounds—the future heartaches and past resentments—we craft our ability to open as a clear and creative channel for our present mission.

GodEsSenz (2007)

CLAY ANGELS

Because
We fall down again
We forgive all debts
Clay angels forget
That we are
God's present

Broken, beloved
Open hearts amend
We came to confess
That we are Luminous

We fall down again
So we forgive all debts.
Clay angels forget
that we are gods
present.

(Follow this LINK http://soundcloud.com/verdarluz to the song)

CHAPTER 10

The Wounded Healer in Popular Culture

Chiron, the Life Coach: The Way of the Mentor

In the first two decades of the 21st century, a major phenomenon has spread worldwide, which not only affects how we relate to each other, but our sense of economy and collective values. This phenomenon revolves around the birth of the Coach as an emerging archetype.

Coaches can be in various domains—life coach, business coach, relationship coach, parenting coach, athletics coach, etc. In fact, there is really no aspect of life where we could not become a coach ourselves, or employ the assistance of one. For instance, everyone who posts any kind of how-to video on Youtube or Vimeo embraces the archetype of the Coach.

Your Secret Niche

The most important aspect of coaching is to first find your particular niche. This is often the area that brings most passion, excitement, and inspiration to your life, something that you already thoroughly enjoy doing every day and would love to help others learn about. Ironically, this same area of passion can often be the area of wounding in your life. That repeated wounding compels you to study and examine this subject or area more, thus, making you more conscious of it in the process. I demonstrate this in the book's appendix in describing Chiron's relationship to other planets in the birth chart. For instance, an individual with the planet Venus contacting Chiron, may consistently find challenge or a sense of victimization in relationships. This suffering will often then compel her to study relationships deeply, and thus, she has the potential of becoming a powerful relationship counselor. Again, this is how the wounds we give ourselves are transmuted from the curse to the gift, both for ourselves and for others.

As the Aquarian economy begins to unfurl before our eyes, we notice that testimonials and reviews of a teacher's information/coaching/style/accuracy, etc. are what fuels others to follow, study, or watch that teacher or artist's material. More and more, each of us are acknowledging the avenues of passion and healing within ourselves and sharing this with others. As we do so, Spirit rewards our service with clients, interest, and financial support in response to what we freely contribute. Shamanic Artists learn to harness their life experience, and then releasing valuable content that benefits others first, thus invoking the mentor or guide.

The activation of this coach also requires learning to identify and speak directly to one's audience. This is the foundational art of mentorship—knowing how to translate your own knowledge in a language that can be understood by the individual or group of people before you. This reminds us of Chiron's hybrid nature, and position astronomically between Saturn and Uranus. Like Chiron we are channeling higher wisdom or cultivating more specific knowledge (Uranus) that must be converted into third dimensional forms for others to grasp (Saturn). In this way, each of us is perpetually coaching another. In doing so, we all become world-bridgers, offering a lens to others which pries open their perceptions to more of the cosmos' creative abundance.

Michael Jackson and Eckhart Tolle: The Chiron Return-Initiation

The Chiron return, which occurs at the ages of 49-50, is one of the most important rites of passage of life. It is an opportunity to shift our personal stories of wounding, to understand them in a greater context of meaning, and to assist others through a process of mentorship. We can step into the higher octave of our life purpose during this critical passage. For instance, during his Chiron return at 50, Eckhart Tolle published *The Power of Now*, which made him an instant international teacher and guide to those seeking transformation and mentorship in their lives.

If we do not answer the invitation at the Chiron return to heal our wounds, we can sometimes dive deeper into the wound, and suffer its fatal potential. This was the case with Michael Jackson, who died within months of his exact Chiron return. His Chiron was in the fourth house of family and upbringing, signifying the pressures and intensity from his father to groom a pop-star at such a young age. His desires to create Neverland and to surround himself with youth spoke of unhealed childhood wounds.

The Wounded Healer in Film

Often, the arts reflect back to us the most profound expressions of an energy awakening in collective consciousness. The medium of film explores the full archetypal panorama of the human emotional experience. Chiron's passage through Pisces (2011-2018) opens the door for all arts, including dance, theater, visual expression, poetry, literature, photography, etc. to share the story of the emerging hero: the Shamanic Artist.

Chiron in Pisces was foreshadowed by his conjunction with Neptune between 2009 and 2011. Like the sign of Pisces, the force of Neptune carries our imaginative yearnings, our longings for redemption, our dreams, our fantasies, through the narratives we all share, most obvious in the art of film. Thus, Chiron, the Wounded Healer was very present in film in those years, with such popular works as *Avatar, Percy Jackson and the Lightning Thief,* the return of *The Karate Kid,* and 2010's Best Picture winner *The King's Speech.*

Avatar

Avatar is a film richly layered with shamanic symbology. It was released the exact day of the Sun aligning with the Galactic Center in 2009. The film takes place on Pandora, in the Alpha *Centauri* star system, linking us to the Centaur symbol. The Alpha Centauri system is the closest solar system to the earth, and is the most frequently referenced in science fiction as possibilities for humanity's first destination once we travel beyond the earth. According to Dr. Paul LaViolette, Alpha Centauri also contains Centaurus A, a galactic center black hole releasing cosmic rays just like our own Milky Way.

In the film, Jake Sully appears wounded from the very first frames of the film, *in a wheelchair*, but confirms the Wounded Healer sentiment, "I told myself that I could pass any test."

Incredibly, Avatar literally borrows the myth of Chiron's wounding by the Hydra's blood on the poisoned arrow. Colonel Miles Quaritch debriefs his soldiers about the "Humanoids called the Na'vi.. they're fond of arrows dipped in a nuerotoxin that will stop your heart in one minute."

Avatar also features the pronounced shamanic symbolism of the horse with the hybrid merger of the bipedal humanoid Na'vi with the eight-legged Direhorse. Suggesting our potential connection with our power animals, the female Na'vi Neytiri has a telepathic bond between her and the animals of the forest.

Jake has many shamanic dreams of flying, which turn out to be gifts of prophecy, since he will later fly atop the pterodactyl-like Toruk.

Avatar also demonstrates our Chiron dilemma at this time: throughout the film, man and machine merge, as well as human and animal. Our shapeshifting, hybrid consciousness and how we choose to integrate these identities is a major theme.

Again, Chiron links the worlds of Saturnian civilization, culture, and the social contract with the liberated and wild spirit of Uranus. "If you want to stay alive, you'll obey the rules," says Saturn figure

Colonel Quaritch. Yet Jake, in his quest for Uranian freedom, for both himself and the Na'vi, rebels against his officers.

Jake's military purpose is to shapeshift into a Na'vi in order to spy on them. Another body, akin to the shaman's spirit-body is created from human DNA mixed with the DNA of the Na'vi. This calls forth some of the major ethical questions of the Aquarian age and the symbolism intrinsic to the 13th sign Ophiuchus (Serpentarius). This sign was based on Chiron's student Asclepius, the Greek god of healing, whose astromythical symbolism instructs us on proper use of scientific power, especially utilizing nano and biotechnology.

Lastly, the "Tree of Souls" is the central figure for the Na'vi people and relates to the Tree of Life on which the shaman travels between dimensions, as well as once again to the DNA code within each living being.

Percy Jackson and the Lightning Thief

Percy Jackson is a young high school student who knows he's a bit different from others. From the earliest scenes, we notice familiar Chironian themes, as Percy's best friend walks with *crutches* and his teacher guides the students through the Greek History museum—*in his wheelchair* (a symbol released in the cinema just months before in another Wounded Healer film: *Avatar*). The crutches and wheelchair reflect the disability which will later be the individuating principle, defining the gifts of these two characters.

Once Percy arrives at Camp Half-Blood his crutched friend is revealed to be a satyr—half man and half goat, a symbol of the hybrid we discussed earlier. At camp, Percy's school teacher turns out to be Chiron, the mentor and wise centaur. It is stunning, and appropriate, that the mythical Chiron should literally appear in a popular Hollywood film when Chiron and Neptune—the planet of film, the arts, and fashionable trends—conjoined in the sky in early 2010.

Percy himself, must realize that he is also a hybrid demi-god. At Camp "Half-Blood," demi-gods train to become leaders, warriors, and heroes. "But," Percy states, "I'm not a hero, I'm a loser. I have dyslexia, ADHD." His friend, the satyr shares with Percy the Chiron instruction: "And those are your greatest gifts. You're impulsive Percy, you can't be still. Those are your natural battle reflexes. They kept you alive in your fight. Your blood is special. It's the blood of a god."

Percy's teacher, Chiron, tells him, "You left the camp and disobeyed my orders...which is why you're my favorite student. You can receive all the training in the world, but ultimately, you'll have to follow your instincts, grace under pressure..." This is exactly the maverick lesson of the renegade bodhisattva, the Wounded Healer, the Shamanic Artist.

Harry Potter

Even the book and film titles of the Harry Potter series are alchemical, shamanic, and Wounded Healer references, including *The Order of the Phoenix, The Half-Blood Prince*, and *The Sorcerer's Stone.* (In alchemy, the Philosopher's Stone was the goal of the entire work, and the phoenix is the mythical bird who rises out of his own ashes).

Both Percy Jackson and Harry Potter play with the important Chiron theme of the exiled hybrid: Harry is an orphaned "half-blood," Percy is a 'half-breed" demi-god, fathered by Poseidon.

In *The Half-Blood Prince*, Harry and his friends drink a potion that almost kills them. This scene has a striking resemblance to a visionary journey with the serpent medicine of Ayahuasca. Beings of the fire and water elements thrash and flail and overwhelm Harry and his friends at the crucial apex of the film.

The King's Speech

In *The King's Speech*, 2011's Academy Awards Best Picture Winner, the Duke of York, played by Academy Award winner Colin Firth, has a speech impediment. He is reluctant to heal and ashamed at his wound. Eventually, the Duke becomes King and must give a speech to inspire and guide the people of the United Kingdom. A speech therapist, the figure of Chiron in the film, appears to guide the King through unorthodox, maverick approaches, just as Chiron taught the great heroes appropriate to their purpose.

The speech therapist, played by Geoffrey Rush, also feels that the Duke could be a great king. He wants to heal him so the king will gain confidence, but the Duke can only choose to heal himself. This point is very instructive for those of us lightworkers today, who must offer their healing work unconditionally, without forcing our perspectives or guidance on those who are unable to yet receive it, whether they be family, friend, lover, or client.

Lastly, the speech therapist is also an actor; and in a riveting scene, we watch him at a casting call, where he is told that he is too old and not talented enough for the part. Thus, he is wounded, unable to fulfill his dreams to be a stage actor. Yet, what he feels deficient in, he offers back in service to the King, and provides him the necessary techniques to deliver a powerful and moving speech to his people. Integrating the personal wound for the purpose of healing another is the major evolutionary imperative of Chiron.

The Karate Kid

During 2010's Chiron-Neptune conjunction, film producers re-released *The Karate Kid,* an iconic film from my childhood in the 80's. In this version however, the young African-American boy moves to China, demonstrating the increased interdependence and crossover of East/West. The young boy must wear the energy of the Chiron outsider and exile. These points highlight the shamanic themes of Chiron to be a worldbridger, dancing in the liminal, in between realms, a wise centaur not quite east, west, not quite human, animal.

When Pat Morita was cast in the original *Karate Kid* in 1982, he was 50 years old, near his exact Chiron return, which made him an ideal conduit to channel the energy of Chiron, the Wounded Healer, which permeates the entire film. First, Daniel, like the figure of Chiron, is without a father. He finds a surrogate father figure in his martial arts mentor and spiritual guide, Mr. Miyagi. But Mr. Miyagi is also wounded, as we witness his suffering in his drunken confession of the loss of his wife and child during World War II. Miyagi's drinking also demonstrates the Wounded Healer's ability and temptation to wound himself.

Miyagi is at first reluctant to offer up his wound in service by teaching a pupil. Like all of us, we often seek to define our separate selves through our wounded aspects. But our healing transpires as we teach *through* the wound. Whether we do bodywork, teach yoga, counsel, coach, or make inspiring art, we must allow ourselves to break open our hearts to let our love spill forth in compassionate instruction for others.

In the riveting scene at the end of Karate Kid, Miyagi introduced western culture to Reiki as he rubbed his palms together to generate the healing Chi, which allowed Daniel to return to the ring to fight. All forms of alternative energetic healing are related to Chiron.

Comic Superheroes

Since the early 2000's, a phenomena has unfolded in the world of film: the obsession with comic superheroes and mythology. This theme will likely continue to dominate Hollywood while Uranus is in heroic Aries through 2018 and Neptune is in mythical Pisces through 2024. We should not underestimate the potency of this phenomena in disseminating the characteristics of the Wounded Healer archetype since most comic superheroes are what we may call "wounded heroes."

First, there is an intrinsic nature of suffering that persists in the lives of superheroes. Often, like Chiron, to become a superhero one must first be exiled or ostracized in some way. The X-Men are supreme examples of this. Like Chiron's unique abilities, skills, and training, each of those recruited to be X-Men have some kind of mutant ability, which simultaneously alienates and empowers them. The similarities to the Wounded Healer/Hero archetype are remarkable: just like in Avatar or Percy Jackson, Professor X is physically wounded: a paraplegic in, once again, a wheelchair. But he is an extremely gifted telepath, able to read, control, and influence human minds. Like Chiron, Professor X trains the young mutants at his hidden home, X-Mansion, resonant with the cave in which Chiron taught the great heroes and healers.

Superheroes, such as the X-Men, are hybrid beings, linking worlds, shamanically bridging the mundane middle world with the underworld unconscious shadow (the arch-enemy) and the ascended upper worlds.

Superman, Batman, Spider-Man, many of the X-Men are also just some of the examples of the *orphaned* superhero, again reverberating themes of Chiron.

To be without family means that many superheroes become *children of the world*. Without familial obligations, the superhero stands, with the world as a parent and all its inhabitants as family. Like the arch-servant Chiron, the superhero then feels a duty to assist or save the entire world. In the case of Batman, for instance, the murder of his parents early in his youth (a childhood wound), then motivates him to make the world safer for other children.

In the *Iron Man* film, Tony Stark is head of Stark Industries, a major military contracting company he inherited from his father. One day while participating in a demonstration of his latest weapon, Stark is critically *wounded*. During this process, he recognizes how he has *wounded* others, decimating populations, through his technological innovation, and determines to help those he has wounded. Also, during his captivity, Stark gains power through an electromagnetic suit, becoming Iron Man. Upon returning home, Stark announces that his company will no longer manufacture weapons. In becoming Iron-Man Stark heals his ancestral baggage, resonating with Chiron's story of ancestral healing with his Grandfather Uranus and his father Saturn, both of whom destroyed their young.

In *Spider-Man*, *Batman*, and other superhero sagas, we also find the shamanic motif of the animal shape-shifter. In Batman, the very thing that Bruce Wayne fears the most—bats—become not only his power animal ally, but the very kind of superhero he morphs into. Carl Jung's idea that we become the very thing we try to avoid is important to elucidate the power which integration of the shadow unconscious can bring into our lives.

Similarly, in the *Spider-Man* film, Peter Parker is bitten by a genetically engineered spider, which then gives him enhanced, spider-like abilities such as wrists which emit web strings, super quick reflexes, and the ability to scale walls and jump between rooftops The bite or wound actually makes him stronger, and ultimately gives him a more bodhisattvic skill—to help all beings by fighting crime.

Lastly, in the *X-Men*, in *Spider-Man*, in *Iron Man*, and other superhero stories, a major theme involving the inappropriate and selfish use of technology consistently emerges. Remembering that Chiron taught the sacred use of weaponry, we see how these superhero themes concern the Wounded Healer's awareness of both the wounding and life-supportive aspects of technology, a fundamental theme of the emerging Aquarian Age.

CHAPTER 11

The Grace of the Wound

The doctor is effective only when he himself is affected. Only the wounded physician heals.

—*Carl Jung*

In this statement, Jung suggests that a malady of the soul could be the best possible form of training for a healer. In fact, as we have discussed in this work, it is *because* of this malady, that one awakens to the healing journey, and eventually a more cosmic and integral sense of self.

This transpersonal self-awareness—the self not confined to role, duty, family, religious system, nor to ego's insatiable hunger for guilt and separation—that transpersonalized self must become aware of its sacred wound as that which teaches us empathy.

This luminous dharma, one's True Nature, fuses the supreme virtues of both Wisdom and Compassion. This is symbolized in Tibetan Buddhism by the Dorje Vajra, the masculine symbol of compassion, and the Bell, the feminine symbol of wisdom.

Epiphany emerges as you, the earthborn initiate, realize that through the suffering experience that repeats, you learn to become compassionate. Your right relationship to the wound is the vehicle carrying you to your wisdom-medicine.

The wound evolves into medicine as the pains and burdens you bear and eventually surmount become the source of great strength, advice, and healing power for others. Jung continues, "The suffering patient can be cared for by the healer and be instrumental in the healer's own healing....Each encounter between healer and patient can be transforming for both."

This sense of 'fatedness' in our wounds recalls the mystery of incarnation itself and the karmas that compel us into our life situations, our relationships, and our experiences. Because we cannot understand the full spectrum of its origin, the ego must surrender its desire to control, and in so doing pry open the heart to the mysterious necessity that all is occurring intentionally in Love's labyrinthine design.

This is the most profound shift that occurs now, in 2012, as this book is published. We have been and will continue to gift ourselves every challenging situation we can handle. And we will continue to attract those angelic messengers, the emanations of Raphael, who require our help, as we require theirs, to nurture the wound with the salve of dedicated service and the prayer of our creative vibrations.

In the appendix, you will find how the sacred wound is offered back in service, depending on what pattern of energy (sign), force of consciousness (planetary intelligence), and area of one's life (house) is affected by Chiron. For some, it is relationships (Venus,) for others home and the maternal principle (Moon). But we all have areas and aspects of our psyche which seek to be overcome with the commitment and disciplined practice of the *Übermensch*. For us today, Nietzsche's Overman has become the Wounded Healer in the mirror. You, Shamanic Artist, perform humble miracles with the grace of the Heavenly Twin. You carry us across the threshold to bask as One, once again, in the Lantern of our Source.

The Silent Metaphor

Towards the end of a shamanic ceremony, during a time period while I was editing this book, I was moving my laptop from one room to another in my home, when I suddenly started to channel a powerful dance *with the computer*.

This dance became an epiphany—a profound and humorous healing began to occur as I hugged the computer to my chest, stroked its lid and body, offered it as a hand model would, wrapped its cord around my neck, and more.

Each gesture became a metaphor for my constant struggle with this repeating wound. The dance took on the texture of miming, and I realized that this dance would be the closing of my book. This visual meditation can be viewed here: http://www.youtube.com/user/verdarluzmagi/videos.

Would the technological wound go away? No. Could I react differently to it? Yes. Could I offer it back as a teaching and guiding story for others? Yes. That is this book, *Aquarius Dawns: the Shamanic Artist and the Rise of the Wounded Healer*. And the resolution of the book, the moment of awakening is this visual meditation, entitled, Umbilicus Alternatio Currente.

The piece encapsulates the spectrum of emotion, from absurdity to awe to disgust, frustration and hopelessness, reunion and triumph, and ultimately, the surrender to the Mystery. Our relationship to the wound often forces us upon the roller coaster, arms held high. It is my hope that the silent mime may symbolize the still and equanimous awareness even as we slalom through the mountains and valleys of our tumultuous, but rewarding healing journey.

EPILOGUE

As I began this book, I wanted to close this work by sharing my personal journey through the Wounded Healer's maze of slow revelation. In doing this, I hope to elucidate some final thoughts on the archetype of the Shamanic Artist.

Earlier, I described the disturbing experience when the speaker fell, due to the bass in my song, onto my laptop's hard drive while I gave a performance. In shock, it felt like I myself had destroyed my own creative tool.

I described this experience with you to demonstrate the wounded complex lurking in my own chart of the planetoid Chiron conjunct the planet Mercury. Mercury rules all technological tools, such as computers, phones, voice recorders, cameras, and cars.

After that "fated," daimonic event, I purchased a new hard drive to install, which helped the computer to function. But over the next month, it would just occasionally, randomly die on me. This occurred throughout the writing of this book.

Eventually I had no choice but to purchase a refurbished computer, since there was permanent damage to that machine. Within just a month of having the new machine, this computer also began to have problems. The monitor would sporadically not turn on when I lifted it, though the computer was still on. There was no way to understand why this was happening.

Then, about six months later, just as I was completing the first draft of this book, and while I was doing a software update on my computer, the computer crashed, and I could not restart it.

In a panic, I called Apple. The disk could not be verified, nor repair itself. The hard drive had failed, *while I was doing a software update?!?!?*

I took it in to Apple. During the repair they replaced the logic board, and shared with me that that there could be water damage. Of course, this "accidental" water damage made me immediately think of what had happened only six months earlier. If there was water damage, apparently I had done something I wasn't aware of, just like playing a song with too much bass so that the vibration would hurdle the speaker onto my laptop.

So what part of my "self" seems to keep inflicting the wound and for what purpose? Is this my daimon, my higher nature, perhaps humbling me, reminding me of some Mysterious forces beyond?

Now the monitor will still randomly not turn on. I have to press some bizarre combination of keys and then put the start-up disk in, and hope it will turn back on. I can bring my computer back in for Apple to test it, but if they cannot duplicate the problem, they will not be able to fix it. Essentially, what this means is that I'll have to accept the tenuous situation with this machine.

I have watched over the years as consistently each of those items Mercury rules—the cars, computers, voice recorders, cameras—have all been broken and lost countless times, a challenging reality to accept for a Gemini rising, ruled by the planet Mercury.

Is this the primary test of my evolution: to see how conscious I have become of my wound? Can I be aware enough to be still and accept its presence, knowing that on some deeper and more transcendent level I cannot fully grasp, this wound is serving me, and helping me to serve others.

When I really dig into it, I realize that the repeating wound compelled me to ask about this wound's origin points. On one level, this motivated me to study the language of the soul—astrology—which has now become my professional service. In addition, my practice and my revelations in Rebirthing breathwork and past life regression therapy owe themselves to the wound. My soul-threads connect me back to a lineage of messengers who lost and fragmented themselves to the story of defeat: of being unable to deliver the message.

It appears that one of my great works in this lifetime is to transcend that limited definition and role of the self as messenger. I now know that as I shift my embodied identification back to its proper place—as the loving essence of the Creator, the Light of the eternal spark—my *role* as a messenger, teacher, or mentor will be fulfilled in the appropriate way, in the appropriate time.

All of us have the task of confronting, entering, and eventually transcending the wounded story. Then the wound can make each one of us a healer, and fashion all of us into a teacher. Thus, the wound is sacred. And now the curse becomes a gift.

LIGHT-HEARTED

I confess:
I am a multidimensional vibration.
But how do I contain that?
I am Being and Becoming
And I am lost and found in the between
All-Ways
But I don't know how to reach the other parts of me,
stretched like melted plastic taffy through wormholes of
possibility.
I am the thirteenth rose, de-thorned, but pricked by the dozen
other red mirrors.
The roses were white, but stained the blood of my zodiacal
reflection.
Archetypes battle in me, and I seek my courage in conjuring
miracles:
the hymns necessary to sustain peace between the gods of war.
And all gods
are gods of war.
And I've been caught stealing
Thunder
I've been caught thieving
Fire
The eagle pecks at my flesh
The swan serenades my soul beyond death
The vulture carries the carrion of my broken heart across the
Milky river Styx
I am the orphan in exile, and I am the hybrid hiding in the cloak of
stars
And my centaur's arrow points back, like an ouroboros tail,
Straight into my mouth—the black hole of the Galactic Core.
I am both Prometheus and the Wounded Healer who spares his
Flame from its famine
I am the Shamanic Artist who sacrifices his heart upon the altar

So that humanity may feast upon dawn for but one more day.
I am the Sacred Face of the Sun
Reaching to kiss you with my Solar Flare lips.
I know my embrace is deadly
But the Light will ascend you
And the Heat will resurrect you
Just stare at me and remember
You are not separate.
Climb into the Light
Return the Many to the One.
And fold the distance
Into Wholeness

Dorje Varja Chrystaliena (2005)

PART 3

LOCATING THE
WOUNDED HEALER:
The Astrological Chiron
by Sign, House, and Aspect

"The practice of Dharma is to pacify the afflictions and concepts that fill our minds...we train in taming our minds. What we tame are the three main afflictions: ignorance, attachment, and aversion."

—*The 17th Karmapa*

When our shadow surfaces, when our wound is revealed, often we will confront it with these three main afflictions. First, we may stay *ignorant* of the wound. We can also *attach* to our wound, in a process of negative identification. The ego wishes to maintain itself, so by fixating to a wounded story, the ego perpetuates its idea of a separate existence. We can also try to *avoid* or *avert* the wound, which will not help us to heal nor give us the tools to help another.

In the language of archetypes, the presence of the Wounded Healer will initiate us into the shamanic hero's journey through Chiron's placement by sign, house, and aspect with other planets. We will locate how we ignore, attach, or try to avert the traumatized aspects of our being.

As the wound, Chiron's placement will show us where we may lack self-esteem, and thereby try to *overcompensate* by proving ourselves in this area. Because of our acute awareness of this seeming lack, we actually gain increased skills and training in this sign where Chiron is, in the house (realm of life experience), and through the planets he is connected to (aspects). Thus through this enhanced attention, as we have described, we can become guides and mentors to others, and fulfill our bodhisattva vow to serve all sentient beings.

Once the wound is no longer used as a way to reinforce the ego's story of separation by instead embracing our bodhisattva vow and serving others in this area, then we ascend in our evolution towards wholeness.

Chiron scholar Melanie Reinhart explains that "The urge to individuate takes on particular urgency for those factors affected by Chiron. There the arrow of the Centaur infuses us with an intensity which often means great suffering, but also indicates the possibility of creating something individual and uniquely our own."

Reinhart further compares the Chiron configuration to *tariqa,* the Sufi concept of one's particular path to God. Like a certain type of yoga, we each have a way of returning to our creator—for some it is devotional practice, for others, intimate love, for some service work, for still others the path of the storyteller or musician. Chiron is an inner teacher whose placements in the chart will reflect the tests, training, obstacles, and disciplines we must follow on our path back to our Source.

When a planet is conjunct, square, or opposite Chiron, it reflects the specific intelligence within us which requires dedicated practice to surmount its challenge. This planetary character functions as the individuating wound, and the healing service.

The flowing trine and sextile aspects to Chiron will be sources of friendly support on our path of integrating the more challenging aspects. They are like our special superpowers which can aid the weaker elements of our being on their path of development.

We should note that relationships with a strong Chiron connection between people—one or both person's Chiron in tight aspects to a partner's personal planets—will reveal deep wounds, emphasizing the role of mentorship, healing, counseling, and compassionate service towards the relationship.

With each **transit of Chiron** or in the sky to our natal chart or **transit to our natal Chiron,** we are catapulted into experiences of being wounded, wounding others, and/or activation of healing skills. This is why many people become compassionate after they experience a tragedy. We cannot learn to heal others until we are actively healing ourselves, and so first we must be wounded, just as Chiron was poisoned in his left leg by an arrow. Unfortunately, what tends to occur when we have been wounded is that we wound others in return. We are so blinded by our own wounds that we often do not see how the pain we feel can be projected onto another.

Chiron transits are ideal times to study the whole of our life and all of our patterns. They are especially poignant opportunities to apply Ho'oponopono—to correct the wrongs in that area by taking the microscope to the planets aspected by Chiron, or aspecting Chiron, and to accept, cleanse, release, pray, and ultimately apply the healing balm of forgiveness to those intelligences within us.

In the section below, you will find descriptions of Chiron in aspect to other planetary forces of consciousness, as well as Chiron in the house and sign which correspond to that planet. Find these connections in your chart to locate the Wounded Healer and Shamanic Artist. Each section closes with a puja, a series of exercises and remedies to assist in the healing of that planet in your life. If you are having Chiron transit one of these planets or houses, or if one of these planets is transiting your Chiron, you can read the following interpretations for guidance as well.

Chiron-Sun; Chiron in the Fifth House or in Leo

With Chiron-Sun aspects, we may feel confused in our goals and purpose and uncertain with our sense of self. Early in life or in other places and times, our unique light may have been buried from unsupportive family, educational environments, or even the wounding of fame. This may have left us feeling invalidated in our self-expression and intimidated to share or oversensitive to criticism.

On the other hand, we may be quite a magnetic and charismatic personality, but not be able to enjoy this fully. In this case, we may feel like we have to be "on show" to receive recognition, yet we may feel estranged from our true self, locked deep within.

There is often shyness with performance and a sense of inadequacy with our creativity. There may be a skill at promoting confidence within others, but completely lacking it in ourselves.

With Chiron-Sun aspects, the image of our father will be colored with Chiron themes—our father may have been absent, wounded, weak, or violent. Alternatively, he may have been a powerful mentor and teacher figure. We may feel competition to shine our light in the way our father did, so we may not adopt the positive attributes he represents.

Women with this contact will often lack the masculine orientations of having set goals and focused means of achieving them.

Thus, they may attach to male figures who have those firmly developed, such as gurus, performers, or more popular personalities.

At our core, this Chiron placement makes us feel an overwhelming need to individuate, to step out and express our unique spark of the life force, without fear of judgment. Yet our ego may have been deflated early on, likely from our parents who may have limited or constricted our free play. Learning to express the inner solar child becomes essential to promoting a healthy ego. We should recreate, play, and experiment with whatever creative paths fulfill us in the moment.

With Chiron in the fifth house or Leo, children may be a source of wounding—perhaps we cannot have them, or they may be ill or handicapped. Yet, much healing can occur from working directly with children, especially supporting their creative play, and helping them establish goals and objectives. Children will reflect the pure expressions of unfettered joy and vital life force that needs to spontaneously express itself in the Chiron-Sun/Chiron fifth house individual.

Sun Puja:

Focus on the thousand-petaled crown chakra, seat of the luminous Absolute. Breathe in silent stillness and know the transcendent being of your Source.

Visualize the solar heroes and deities—Christ, Buddha, Horus, Ahau, Inti.

In Yoga, practice Sun Salutation, Surya Namaskar, preferably at sunrise/sunset.

Chant the Sun mantra: Om hreem surya namah daily or do a Sun puja on Sunday.

Chiron-Moon;
Chiron in the Fourth House or in Cancer

With Chiron-Moon aspects, the emotions can be very awkward to express, or may be tools of manipulation. We may tell ourselves and other that we feel fine when we do not and then expect others to understand. When they do not respond in the appropriate way, we act resentfully towards them.

The process of sharing emotions can be overly dramatic and undulating as the feelings may flow out and overwhelm the self and others, or they may be repressed for fear of any secure container for them.

With this Chiron placement, we often had to take on a mothering role early in life, and may not have been able to nurture ourselves or honor our own needs. Such is the case with some women who have this placement, who become "supermoms," to many children or all her children's friends. But in this act of helping others, she creates incredible anxiety and unsettled energy in her own life.

With Chiron in the fourth house or Cancer, the home environment may have felt unsafe, the foundations unstable, and the family structure itself may have shifted frequently. Thus, this created a deep and penetrating feeling of core insecurity, that the support of our basic needs may not be met.

Mother may have been wounded, sick, or emotionally unavailable, instilling a feeling of abandonment early on. This placement also indicates the possibility of a strong birth-trauma imprint, which made us distrust this world. Early mothering may be our primary wound, such as not receiving the proper nourishment. For instance, we may not have been breast-fed and lack any deep connection to our mother, or even the sense of earth as mother.

Because of the lack of early security in our life, we may perpetually feel "homeless" in our adult life, without a sense of belonging to a particular home, community, or place. On the other hand, we may have a deep desire to return to the womb, to our home of origin, and we may be able to create very healing and nurturing homes for others. We will also have natural gifts of empathy, nurturing, and caregiving, often knowing better how to nourish another than ourselves.

Men with this Chiron placement may be completely cut off from their emotions and reflective abilities, and thus play out macho masculine roles of dominance and control with the women in their lives. On the other hand, men may be highly attuned to the emotions of their mothers, and may spend much of their life caring for them. They will often consistently seek for a maternal figure, especially in their intimate partners. They may choose women who are very caring mothers. The men may feel a competition with those children for Mother's love. But they are healed by becoming nurturing parental figures themselves. They can often be more connected with the inner world and cultivate a stronger psychic intuition than other males.

With Chiron-Moon aspects, Chiron in Cancer, or Chiron in the fourth house, inner child healing work and rebirthing work can provide containers for establishing safety and security in this world, and allowing emotions to express themselves in healthy ways. Crying may be very therapeutic. Letting our emotions express freely, without attachment to them is the great work.

Moon Puja:

Focus on the double-petaled indigo lotus of Ajna, the third eye. Chant its seed syllable Aum

In Yoga, practice Half-Moon and Child's Pose.

Visualize the great mother archetypes—Kuan Yin, Mother Mary, Tara, Durga

Chant the Moon mantra: Om hreem chandraye namah daily or do a Moon puja on Monday, as well as the New and Full Moon.

Chiron-Mercury;
Chiron in Third House or in Gemini
Chiron in Sixth House or in Virgo

With Chiron-Mercury aspects, we must learn to use our words consciously and constructively, towards self and others, as they can be used destructively or in wise guidance. Yet we may doubt our ability to accurately or completely communicate.

In other lifetimes, we may have had an important message to

share and either could not deliver it on time, or our message was ignored, or we were killed for the communication we delivered.

Thus, writing can be a form of therapy. In addition, teaching about a diversity of healing arts can be a natural gift.

Technology can be a primary source of wounding, yet it will likely play a more essential role in the life of the Chiron-Mercury person. It becomes extra important to prepare and plan for Mercury retrograde cycles by backing up important documents and assessing one's mental pursuits and challenges.

With Chiron-Mercury, we may feel as if the trickster himself is teasing us constantly. You must learn to trick the trickster by developing a sense of humor, and learning the arts of adaptation and shapeshifting.

In the third house or Gemini, sibling rivalries may occur. We should give attention to what occurred in our early upbringing. How did our sibling connections or early education possibly prevent the full expression of ourselves?

We may need to examine how we work with information, marketing, and networking, in order to share our message with the world. Does the information and knowledge we attain overwhelm us or liberate us, allowing us to translate our message to anyone? The Buddhist notion of Right Speech is important to adopt. Saying what one means, meaning what one's says. This will be the mark of the Mercurial mentor.

Mercury Puja:
Focus on the blue throat chakra and chant its seed syllable Ham. Visualize Hermes, Mercury, Thoth, or Iris, all messenger deities.

In Yoga, practice all kinds of mantras to open the throat. Especially, chant the Mercury mantra: Om hreem buddhaye namah daily or do a Mercury puja on Mercury's day—Wednesday.

Chiron-Venus;
Chiron in Seventh House or in Libra
Chiron in Second House or in Taurus

With the Chiron-Venus placement, our relationships must promote healing and spiritual growth. We have an acute sensitivity, most likely developed in childhood, to disharmony in relationships. We may also feel repeatedly rejected by others. Thus, we may overcompensate by pretending to be someone we are not in order to attract or remain in a relationship.

We may also idealize relationships, and thus not see them clearly, choosing to hide behind the mask of politeness and grace, when the heart's gritty truth is anger or disillusionment.

We also become acutely aware of physical beauty and how it can be used to manipulate all kinds of relationships. Thus, Chiron-Venus individuals may develop distorted versions of relationship—co-dependent or trapped by the material facade of pleasures and luxury.

Instead of vanity or living up to images, we must discover our worth within ourselves, and create our own sense of aesthetic appreciation, which will in turn, be naturally beautiful to others. Artistic and musical practices assist in this process.

With Chiron-Venus, Chiron in the seventh house, or Chiron in Libra, betrayal and abandonment may have occurred in other lifetimes, and so we we will consistently attract partners who will force us to open and trust. On a deeper level, we must awaken to our intrinsic worthiness as a living spirit. We my feel a deep familiarity with each of our partners, magnetizing many soul-mates and mentors, who require us to transform ourselves in our interactions with them. When presented with partnership we may judge or scrutinize immediately, perceiving the lack. Yet, we can also cultivate the heart of compassionate listening.

We can instantly perceive the lack or weakness another may feel and will become aware of how we too lack inner value. Thus, we must be careful not to simply connect with others because of the wounds we share. But instead, we must develop our empathic nature, becoming the spiritual friend to many.

A dynamic dialogue must unfold between oneself and one's partners, so that unconscious forces do not dominate the connection. It is important to ask, "Am I playing the role of wonder, victim, or healer? How can this relationship teach me to rise above over-identification with any of those roles? Can we strike the delicate balance between my needs and my partner's?

Because of the sensitivity to the other, Chiron-Venus, Chiron in the 7th house or Chiron in Libra individuals can make ideal relationship coaches and counselors. They will also be adept at many artistic skills and practices where energy balance is essential, such as feng shui.

With Chiron in Taurus or the second house, we may feel a disconnection from the sensual world. There may have been little to no affection growing up or we may have lacked a relationship to nature growing up and feel overwhelmed by the experience of returning to the embodied world. The physical body itself may feel unstable or may be physically damaged in some way. Dance, cooking, gardening, hiking, and music can be activities which return us to the immediate pleasures of our senses and appreciation of our earthly existence.

A lack of self-confidence and material instability may plague us. In this lifetime or others, we may have been quite impoverished, or on the other hand, money may have been such a priority that we either become quite possessive or abhor ownership of things.

The goal is to build one's own personal value system, discovering what is important to oneself. This requires trusting the instinctual body and developing one's own concepts of beauty, regardless of cultural concepts.

Venus Puja:
Focus on the green heart chakra Anahata and chant its seed syllable Yam.

In Yoga, practice Balance poses, such as Tree pose.

Visualize Aphrodite, Lakshmi, Cupid, or any other god/goddess of love.

Chant the Venus mantra: Om hreem shukraye namah daily or do a Venus puja on Venus' day—Friday.

Chiron-Mars;
Chiron in the First House or in Aries

Our early childhood environment may have been exposed to the negative expressions of Mars—violence, aggression, battle, and confrontations. Thus, we could repeat this wound with others, acting with cruelty, harshness, or physical abuse. On the other hand, asking for what we want and asserting ourselves may not only challenge us, but bring fear at the possibly violent consequences. We may lack confidence in expressing our desires, or feel shame when we do, doubting whether they are valid.

There can be a passive-aggressive quality that may make us compulsively act without thinking, or in the reverse, may make us attempt to control situations by not taking actions. We can use getting sick as an unconscious way of manipulating and asserting some element of will.

In other lifetimes, we will have likely been either the victim or perpetrator of violence or aggressive force. We may consistently magnetize lovers, friends, employees, and family members in whom we trigger an explosive reaction. This will force us to confront the element of fire and ask ourselves how we truly wish to tend the flame of our passions.

Yet, as we attune ourselves to the 'fire in our belly,' we become aware of our potential to lead and accomplish almost anything. Intelligent and strategic use of our energy can develop the archetype of the General. We can think of the Tai Chi master, whose sensitivity to chi makes him ten times stronger than any man since he can use another's force against him.

Martial arts, dance, weightlifting, and sports should be adopted as a spiritual path, as they can help release pent up energy and frustration, as well as challenge one to ignite the will and self-determination, thereby building self-confidence.

With Chiron in Aries or near the Ascendant, or placed in the first house, we can strongly identify with the archetype of the Wounded Healer. Because of this, we may repeatedly experience existential crises, even questioning life's worth. In addition, our spontaneous expressions as a child may have been suppressed. Thus, with this placement, we will need to develop a path of healthy and motivating service in our life, wearing the mask of the mentor in our daily life.

It is essential that people with Chiron-Mars, Chiron in the first, or Chiron in Aries, discover a mission for themselves which can energize, realize, and focus their inner fire.

Mars Puja:

Focus on the golden downward-facing triangle of the third chakra, the will center Manipura, and chant its seed syllable Ram.

In Yoga, practice the Warrior postures.

Visualize the spiritual warrior, the martial arts master.

Chant the Mars mantra: Om hreem mangala namah daily or do a Mars puja on Mars' day—Tuesday.

Chiron-Jupiter;
Chiron in the Ninth House or in Sagittarius

With contacts between Chiron and Jupiter, our wound will likely involve some amount of overconfidence that leads to extreme behavior or belief systems. We may dogmatically assert a philosophy or religious ideal, and then experience a crisis of faith when we experience misfortune or loss. We may feel rage when our boundless optimism meets with an experience of limitation.

Instead of overconfidence, we may also experience the opposite—a sense of hopelessness, a lack of trust, or little faith in the abundance of life. This usually occurs because of an experience in childhood which devastated the sense of generosity, abundance, or meaning. There may have been some great loss or lack of religious faith at all in our parent's lives, which they then transmitted to us as extreme caution and suppression. Joy, luck, and the divine order may have been foreign or threatening concepts. This then may compel us towards an extended and perilous quest, seeking some semblance of meaning through our own experience.

In another lifetime, we may have put all our faith in a religious teacher only to become disillusioned or traumatized. Thus, we may in this life, negate the spiritual path or any element of divine timing. On the other hand, we may become messianic with our own message, somewhat fanatic, excessive, or zealous with a particular perspective, which can become a battleground when challenged by others.

With Chiron-Jupiter, Chiron in Sagittarius, or Chiron in the 9th, we are often drawn towards experiences of travel, journey, and pilgrimage which can bring meaning and larger understanding. But the crucial factor is how willing and able we are to integrate the spiritual lessons and expanded perspectives which such quests provide. If we do not stop to process, we can victimize ourselves by becoming addicted to experience, without understanding the meaning behind them.

Often holy places—ashrams, shrines, temples—and the more exotic customs of foreign cultures nourish our souls. We are drawn to gurus and lineages, and if we integrate the vast panorama of our voyage, we can become great teachers and storytellers of philosophy, theology, cosmology, and mythology.

Jupiter Puja:

Focus on the orange half-moon and diamond of the second chakra, the creative Swadhistana, and chant its seed syllable Vam.

In Yoga, practice Nataraja, the cosmic dancer, and point outward towards your goals.

Visualize the guru of your spiritual path, an inspiring world teacher such as the Dalai Lama, or an empowering personal teacher you have had.

Chant the Jupiter mantra: Om hreem brihaspatye namah daily or do a Jupiter puja on Jupiter's day—Thursday.

Chiron-Saturn;
Chiron in the Tenth House or in Capricorn

With Chiron-Saturn placements, we must negotiate the father-principle in the world. Either we feel constrained by the pressures to achieve, and suffer the judgements if we do not, or we may feel feeble in our worldly roles, depressed, or lacking the ability to strategize, work hard, and build enduring structures in our life.

Often our father figure plays an important role in our lives—perhaps he was unknown, weak and incapable, or exerted a rigid authoritarian energy over us. With Saturn and Chiron together, there is often a need to study our ancestral lineage, especially from the father's side, to uncover the inheritance of the burdens and responsibilities through our genetic line. The strict upbringing and ancestral storyline may make us feel like we have to take on struggles which are not even our own. Our healing comes in unveiling the conservative and rigid attitudes we have inherited, letting our defenses down, allowing emotions to surface, and doing only that work which is personally fulfilling.

We may also become serious at a young age and grow up before our time, lacking an ability to be emotionally vulnerable. This may in turn lead us to becoming tyrannical, controlling, or judgmental with others.

With Chiron in the tenth house of Capricorn, we may be uncertain of our ambitions or have any sense of what true success may feel like. Our vocational goals may be unclear. Alternatively, we may be perceived as quite successful or respectable, but not enjoy our achievements, or often feel like we must still accomplish more, thus suffering to our own impossibly high standards.

These standards were likely imprinted in us from our early upbringing, or in other lifetimes, from distinct hierarchical structures and institutions such as the military. These may create an overwhelming pressure to prove our self-worth, and compel us to become obsessed with achieving status. On one end, we may appear to lack accountability, while on the other hand we may overextend ourselves and try to be responsible for areas which are out of our control.

Finding a vocation which feels meaningful and provides an opportunity to lead others is part of the healing path with Chiron-Saturn, 10th house, or in Capricorn. We must through our trials and hard work, discover our own inner authority. This will in turn radiate outwardly towards others as the archetype of the tribal elder, filled with dignity, integrity, and wisdom.

Saturn Puja:

Focus on the red square of the root chakra, Mooladhara, and chant its seed syllable, Lam.

In Yoga, practice Mountain pose, standing still. Attune to the bones and strengthen the skeletal system.

Visualize the wise and respected elder.

Chant the Saturn mantra: Om hreem shreem shanaischaraya namah daily or do a Saturn puja on Saturday.

Chiron-Uranus;
Chiron in the 11th House or in Aquarius

The contact between Uranus and Chiron is not unique, as Chiron's orbit opposed Uranus forty exact times between 1952 and 1989. Collectively, this era has been a profound initiation, sparking much of the rebellious and revolutionary fervor over this time period, as individuals have sought to maximize personal freedom, both politically and in concepts of reality, through computer based technological advancement and a new perception on reality with quantum physics.

Chiron-Uranus individuals perceive uniquely. They take every currently existing thing and can innovate and improve upon it. Often ahead of their time, they may be ostracized for their brilliance or paradigm-shifting ideas. There is a strong desire to rebel against all rigid forms and limiting structures, not necessarily with an alternative system that can be grounded in form or implemented by others.

Authorities are often perceived as enemies, and there can be an adolescent sense of rebellion for its own sake, without any inner truth or more cosmic perspective. Likewise, with Chiron in Aquarius or the 11th house, one may get lost in the frenzy of a collectivist movement and lack any personal center. The ideals of our affiliated groups, whether political or otherwise, may negate our own personal truth.

We must cultivate a rational and discriminating quality in our own minds, which allow us to revolt against any thinking which does not free or liberate ourselves and others. With this placement, we must act as world-bridgers between the dominating and inflowing paradigms, promoting social and cultural evolution, without toppling all of the world's structures.

Uranus Puja:
Focus on third eye, seat of intuition.

In Yoga, practice the upside-down postures, such as Wheel, Bridge, Headstand, and Shoulderstand.

Visualize lightning bolts, electricity, and the rebellious, inventive quality of the titan Prometheus, stealing fire from the gods.

Chiron-Neptune;
Chiron in the 12th House or in Pisces

With Chiron-Neptune contacts, there is close contact to the spirit world, the domain of dreams, and the realm of the imagination. We receive wounds as our fantasies are ruptured, specifically of the sense of unity which weaves us all together. The state of merger with our divine source or our fantasy is severed when third dimensional reality creeps in to set up boundaries and exclusivities, in turn disillusioning, depressing, or confusing us.

Conflict is very hard to handle and we may collapse under the mode of victimization. The belief in the perfected realms of the spirit world can make one naive or easily deceived in dealing with those with darker agendas.

Early in our lives, the longing for unity may display itself through escapist means of intoxication such as alcohol or drugs, in self-destructive behavior, or in an inability to deal responsibly with worldly affairs. The already fragile ego can become even more fractured and drowned in chaos if one does not have some more disciplined, daily practice.

With this placement, however, intentional alteration of one's consciousness can produce a profound shamanic awareness of the multidimensional self. The meditative consciousness can then pry the artistic channel wide open. Thus, literature, poetry, film, music, dance, theater, and mythology are comfortably navigated as creative gifts and healing outlets.

With Chiron in Pisces or the 12th house, an acute psychic awareness develops that can both assist others, but also encroach upon any personal boundaries we may have.

Thus, we may develop a sense of envy for those who have a more pronounced sense of personal identity, since we can be overwhelmed in an oceanic wave of archetypal awareness or connection with the spirit world. Thus, we can feel gripped by gods and forces far beyond our control. This can also occur through overpowering dream experiences, which often feel more real than waking reality. Entities— from vampiric astral forms to power animals—may enter the dream space, and we have the ability to develop a prophetic and healing capacity with our dreams.

At times, we may feel martyred, as though we must redeem others and sacrifice ourselves in the process. We may naturally be drawn towards institutions such as prisons and hospitals to offer our service.

Your highly empathic nature means that you must allow for consistent quiet reflection, meditation, or retreat. Isolation may be necessary as a means to protect oneself. The goal is to establish a connection to nature, the imagination, and our spiritual essence in a healthy balance with responsible action in the world.

Neptune Puja:

Focus on the light-body, breathing a ball of light through every part of the body.

In Yoga, rest in corpse pose, practice Tibetan dream of sleep yoga, and *yoga nidra*—conscious deep sleep for extreme relaxation and subtler spiritual exploration.

Visualize the angelic realms, perhaps archangel of healing Raphael and other spirit guides and power animals. Visualize or meditate upon a paradise or heavenly realms. Imagine the buddhas and bodhisattvas depicted in the Tibetan Buddhist mandalas.

Sit in silence and utter stillness, or chant Tat Twam Asmi—Thou art That. Simply be and receive.

Chiron-Pluto;
Chiron in Eighth House or in Scorpio

With the Chiron-Pluto contact, deep feelings, often from pre-verbal times, may resurface through intimate and sexual relationships, bringing catharsis and turmoil. The shadow emotions—jealousy, greed, envy, possessiveness, control, rage—must be confronted and transmuted alchemically. The life is a deeply psychological one and one benefits from the study of Carl Jung, the archetypes, alchemy, and the shadow.

There is likely an obsessive draw towards power and complexity—emotionally, financially, sexually. One can become incredibly secretive, fearing the overwhelming vulnerability and intensity of the emotional experience.

With Chiron-Pluto, we can feel a strong resonance with the spiritual trials of indigenous shamans, experiencing a sense that we too are in constant initiation and transformation. Thus, these individuals naturally attune to their instinctual selves and develop reservoirs of resilience amidst storm and suffering.

With Chiron in the 8th house or Scorpio, sexuality itself can feel consistently wounding, often related to early experiences of incest or abuse. The sexual act may be experienced as both death and rebirth. Sexual healing and tantric awareness can be liberating tools of self-revelation, and connection with the Source.

We may have experienced death early on in our lives through family or loved ones, and we have the distinct sense of mortality and the fragility of existence. With this placement, we may even feel drawn to end our own lives. There can be an impending sense of catastrophe, a lack of trust in anything or anyone. Often, this feeling originates in unconscious trauma, such as the birth trauma or repressed energy from past lives. Thus rebirthing, breathwork, past life therapy, shamanic healing, and psychotherapy can be necessary tools for unlocking the unconscious trauma within a safe container.

Because of the depth of personal analysis and the acute awareness of the more subtle emotions, Chiron-Pluto, 8th house, or Chiron in Scorpio individuals can make excellent therapists, able to penetrate to the core of any issue, and hold space for the darker extremes of the human experience. Ultimately, these individuals learn to accept what is as it is.

Pluto Puja:

Focus on the dan tien, the hara, the energy center which is the cauldron of your being located near the navel, between the second and third chakra.

In Yoga, do breath of fire; practice other modes of breathwork and past life therapy.

Visualize the dark, serpent goddesses of transformation, including Kali, Lillith, Pele, Hecate, and Inanna

Chant Kali's mantra to purify the shadows:

Krim krim krim hum hum hrim hrim daksine
kalike krim krim krim hum hum hrim hrim svaha

Chiron-Nodes

The Nodes are the karmic axis in the birth chart, representing inheritance from other lifetimes and ancestry. The South Node reflects patterns, tendencies, and habits in the soul, as well as gifts and developed qualities which can be offered to others. It is the path of least resistance, but also, least growth. The North Node symbolizes the soul's path of evolutionary development and spiritual fulfillment. We can often be "hungry" in this area, and feel simultaneously unfamiliar and awkward in this unchartered territory, since this point is opposite where we have been accustomed to.

With Chiron conjunct either node, our lives are strongly colored by Chironian themes. The archetypes of the victim, sacrificial lamb, orphan, savior, redeemer, wise teacher, counselor, and coach will strongly pulse through us. If our healing journey remains unconscious in us, the element of the "wounding one" may dominate our lives and relationships. But if we confront our suffering and alchemically offer back the wisdom of our sacred wounds, we can become profound healers for others.

We may be drawn to working with the disabled or into all fields associated with healing and counseling. There will likely be an attraction to a guru or mentor figure which can guide one's self-actualization and individuating process—a fundamental desire of the Chiron-Node connection.

If Chiron is conjunct your South Node, you incarnate with both a sense of some primal wound deeply imprinted, as well as natural healing gifts to offer others. Lifetimes as a shaman, healer, or teacher are likely.

If Chiron is conjunct your North Node, there is a strong need to develop the capacity to confront your wounds and step into your role as a healer and guide for others. There will be mentor figures who appear in your life to awaken your consciousness and show you the way of the wounded healer.

If Chiron squares the Nodes, we must confront the wounds and limitations which feel like such an obstacle in our lives. The archetype of the wounded healer acts as a threshold guardian for one's evolution in this lifetime, and its integration may have been blocked or stunted in other places and times.

Summon the Master Within!
The Immaculate Perception
of the Wounded Healer

Nothing that I experience is caused by anything outside of me.
I experience only the effects of my own choice.

Shamanic Artist:
"What have you done to overcome yourself lately?"
How have you cracked the caged limitations of your shell?

I am pure spirit, undefiled and unaffected
by anything or anyone.
I am given full power to choose and, therefore,
to create my experience as I would have it to be.

Artist, if you would create well, ask only:
What am I committed to communicating?
What will my creations express?
What will my creations convey to others?

For what I seek to convey reveals
what I believe is the truth of myself and the world.

This is my Choose-My-Own-Adventure!

I vow to become the master of my Spirit
and the mediator of my Soul.

I will contact dance with my Shadow.
I will kiss the Serpent's lips.
I will wrestle with the wound.

I will heal
the broken, open heart.

Geometric Zodiamorph (2006)

VISIONARY SHAMANIC ARTIST
REFERENCES

Romio Shrestha. romioshrestha.com
David Heskin. www.newskinstudio.com
Adam Scott Miller. www.corpuscallosum.cc
Aloria Weaver. www.aloriaweaver.com
Krystle Smith. krystleyez.com
Amanda Sage. amandasage.com
Ben Barta. www.jogegarts.com
Stevee Postman. www.stevee.com
Autumn Skye Morrison. AutumnSkyeMorrison.com
Eric Nez. EricNez.com
Jah Ishka Lah. ishkanexus.com
Andrew Jones. androidjones.com
Carey Thompson. www.galactivation.com
Luke Brown. spectraleyes.com
Roman Villagrana. artbyroman.com
Robert Donaghey. artisticgenius.com
Alex Grey. alexgrey.com
Pablo Amaringo. pabloamaringo.com
Martina Hoffman. martinahoffman.com
Robert Venosa. venosa.com
Dan Cohen. dc-creativelabs.com
Casey Greenling. www.flickr.com/photos/heartofgreenling
VerDarLuz. soulalchemyastrology.com

And many more...

BIBLIOGRAPHY

BOOKS

Andrews, Ted. *The Animal-Wise Tarot*. Jackson, TN: Dragonhawk Publishing, 2007.

Arroyo, Stephen. *The Astrology of Transformation*. Sebastopol, CA: CRCS Publications, 1978.

Barnstone, William and Marvin Meyer, eds. *The Gnostic Bible*. Boston, MA: Shambhala, 2003.

Brezny, Rob. *The Televisionary Oracle*. Berkelley, CA: North Atlantic, 2000.

Capra, Fritjof. *The Tao of Physics*. London: Flamingo Harpercollins; 3rd edition 1992.

Clow, Barbara Hand. *The Eye of the Centaur*. Rochester, Vermont: Bear and Co, 1989.

Corbin, Henry. *The Man of Light in Iranian Sufism*. Boulder and London: Shambala, 1978.

Dennis, Sandra Lee. *Embrace of the Daimon*. York Beach, ME: Weiser Books, 2001.

Diamond, S. A. *Anger, madness, and the daimonic*. Albany, NY: State University of New York Press, 1996.

Dodds, *Pagan and Christian in an Age of Anxiety*. Cambridge, England: Cambridge University Press, 1991.

Edinger, Edward F. *Anatomy of the Psyche: Alchemical Symbolism in Psychotherapy.*

The Idiot's Guide to Alchemy. 1985. La Salle, Illinois: Open Court.

Hancock, Graham. *Supernatural.* New York. The Disinformation Company, 2007.

Harpur, Patrick. *The Philosopher's Secret Fire: A History of the Imagination.* 2002. London: Ivan R. Dee.

Hauck, Dennis William. *The Complete Idiot's Guide to Alchemy.* NY: Penguin, 2008.

—*The Emerald Tablet: Alchemy for Personal Transformation.* NY: Penguin Compass, 1999.

Jenkins, John Major. *Galactic Alignment: The Transformation of Consciousness According to Mayan, Egyptian, and Vedic Traditions.* Rochester, Vermont: Bear and Co., 2002.

Das, Lama Surya. *Letting Go of the Person You Used To Be.* NY: Three Rivers Press, 2004.

Kaufman, Walter, ed. *The Portable Nietzsche.* NY: Penguin, 1976.

Peake, Anthony. *The Daemon: A Guide to Your Extraordinary Secret Self.* London: Arcturus, 2008.

Reinhart, Melanie. *Chiron and the Healing Journey.* London: Penguin, 1989.

Rasha. *Oneness.* Santa Fe: Earthstar Press, 2003.

Tarnas, Richard. *Cosmos and Psyche: Intimations of a New World View.* Viking, New York, NY, 2006.

VerDarLuz. *Codex of the Soul: Astrology as a Spiritual Practice, Vol. 1 The STARchetyapl Theater.* Evergreen, CO: Theophany Publishing, 2010.

Wilber, Ken. *A Spectrum of Consciousness*. Wheaton, IL: Quest Books, 1993

Schuchman, Helen. *A Course in Miracles: Combined Volume*. Foundation for Inner Peace. Mill Valley, 2007.

Woolger, Roger J. *The Story of the Heart*. NY: Published by the Author, 2008.

Ryan, Robert. *The Strong Eye of Shamanism: A Journey into the Caves of Consciousness*. Rochester, Vermont: Inner Traditions, 1999.

AUDIO

Gainsburg, Adam. "Chiron." Lecture at the Blast Astrology Conference, 2008.

Ray, Sondra. Rebirthing Breathwork Intensive Workshop, Ft. Lauderdale, FL, 2009.

INTERNET

James, Tad. "What is Huna?" http://www.ancienthuna.com/ho-oponopono.htm

LaViolette, Dr. Paul. "Cosmic Rays."

http://www.youtube.com/watch?v=3CP9WKmKeLQ -

The Nazarene Way of Essenic Studies. "My God, Why Hast Thou Forsaken Me?" http://www.thenazareneway.com/why_hast_thou_forsaken_me.htm

Henry David Thoreau Quotes. http://www.brainyquote.com/quotes/authors/h/henry_david_thoreau.html

Freedman, Andrew. "Hot Summer of 2011 Rewrites Record Books, http://www.climatecentral.org/blogs/a-record-hot-summer-interactive-map/

"The Wounded Healer." http://www.youtube.com/watch?v=orxEawi9qro

"The Shadow." http://psikoloji.fisek.com.tr/jung/shadow.htm

Zeitgeist: Addendum. zeitgeistmovie.com

IMAGES in ORDER of APPEARANCE

Aquarius Constellation. Hevelius, Johannes. *Uranographia*, 1690.

Aquarius Symbol. http://www.bemyastrologer.com/aq2.jpg

Chiron Symbol. http://www.elsaelsa.com/astrology/2010/11/08/introduction-to-chiron/

Chiron Teaches Achilles the Lyre. Pompeii fresco. http://www.sandanart.com/pwp.html

Mystic vision. Boehme, Jakob. *Theosophische Werke.* http://www.members.shaw.ca/cgjung/Images/Eye.jpg

Calcinatio. Maier, Michael. *Atalanta Fugiens.* Frankfurt, 1618.

Dissolutio. Maier, Michael. *Atalanta Fugiens.* Frankfurt, 1618.

Separatio. Maier, Michael. *Atalanta Fugiens.* Frankfurt, 1618.

Manjushri. http://s157.photobucket.com/albums/t42/thangka/?action=view&current=mani1896.jpg&newest=1

Archangel Michael of Palekh (Unknown Russian painter). http://commons.wikimedia.org/wiki/File:Archangel_Michael_of_Palekh.jpeg

Coniunctio. *Rosarium Philosophorum*. Frankfurt, 1550. http://murraycreek.net/blog/

Asclepius. Museum of Epidaurus Theatre. http://commons.wikimedia.org/wiki/File:Asklepios_-_Epidauros.jpg

Archangel Raphael. Jastrow. 12th-century mosaic La Martorana, Palermo, Italy

http://commons.wikimedia.org/wiki/File:St_Raphael_La_Martorana_Palermo_2008-08-27.jpg

The Medicine Buddha. http://www.thubtenchodron.org/Retreat/index.html

Dorje Vajra and Bell. Mollerup, Asger. "Vajra: A Literature Study," 2002. http://www.sundial.thai-isan-lao.com/sundial_vajra_literature.html

Hermes Trismegistus. Boissard, Jean-Jacques. *De Divinatione et Magicis Praestigiis*, Oppenheim 1616.

ART by VERDARLUZ

Lungs of Life (2007).

The Temple of the Winged Heart (2012).

Halo (2006).

Psila Merkaba (2006).

InfiniTree (2007).

Tikal Hunab Ku: The Shaman's Stairway (2006).

Dorje L.A. (2010).

The Hidden Captain (2005).

AncesTree (2006).

Interdaimonsional (2005).

Redemption Song (2005).

Purnata (2005).

Shamanifest (2006).

GodEsSenz (2007).

Droje Vajra Chriystalien (2005).

Hermes Trismegistus, shamanic master of all worlds, releases the warlike and separatist ego of the lower self, to wield the astrolabe, the book of wisdom, and his caduceus of healing medicine: symbols of his connection to the powers of the above and the soul's return to wholeness.

CLIENT AND STUDENT TESTIMONIALS

"VerDarLuz has given us a world of insight into our 2 yr old. His readings have given us knowledge that our little one could never have verbalized—about his learning style, strengths and weaknesses, and ways to help him thrive in partnership with us. I often refer back to the readings, discovering new gems each time that help me understand and communicate with him. I would encourage anyone interested to begin this precious journey with Ver."

—Jamie Burke, Denver

"I hope one day, in my own astrological craft, I can affect someone with this much profundity and essentially validate their state of being, in the way your words do to me. Your deep insights are so brilliantly synchronous to my inner experience."

—Sabrina Ourania Kheradmand, West Virginia

"VerDarLuz weaves together the major aspects of astrology in such a skillful and interesting way that at last I've been able to make sense of and absorb the information. One may learn much about devotion to purpose by attending his classes and performances."

—Mary Wheeler, Madison, WI

VerDarLuz reflects a spark of the eternal flame as a multimedia artist, integral healer, and author living in Evergreen, CO. He began his healing training in 2003 with courses in Zen Shiatsu, Thai massage, Reiki and Qikung during a 9 month pilgrimage through Asia. He began his studies in astrology shortly after returning, by investigating the Mayan Calendar and working with Mayan elders in Guatemala. His astrological training includes work in the schools of archetypal, Shamanic Astrology, soul-centered Evolutionary Astrology, and Relocation Astrology. In 2009, his work expanded to include Past Life Regression Therapy and Rebirthing Breathwork.

VerDarLuz works closely with coaching and consulting clients and teaches regular teleseminar and webinar courses, including the *Art of Partnership*. He leads Experiential Astrology workshops both nationally and internationally. His workshops also include theatrical performances and sound healing experiences as a DJ, composer, and live musician.

He is the author of *Codex of the Soul: Astrology, Archetypes, and Your Sacred Blueprint*. For coaching, consultations, teaching, and arts, visit him at soulalchemyastrology.com

Lightning Source UK Ltd.
Milton Keynes UK
UKOW05f2133130114

224542UK00004B/439/P